Mordecai
Richler

Mordecai Richler

Edited and with an Introduction by
G. DAVID SHEPS

MICHAEL GNAROWSKI, Series Editor

RYERSON PRESS
McGRAW-HILL COMPANY OF CANADA LIMITED
TORONTO · MONTREAL · NEW YORK · LONDON · SYDNEY
JOHANNESBURG · MEXICO · PANAMA · DÜSSELDORF · SINGAPORE
RIO DE JANEIRO · KUALA LUMPUR · NEW DELHI

MORDECAI RICHLER

ISBN 0-7700-0321-4

For Shelley

CONTENTS

INTRODUCTION

In their themes and motifs, Mordecai Richler's novels
return regularly to a constant set of preoccupations.
Despite this consistency, however, his career as a novelist
has undergone some interesting alterations in terms of his
moral attitudes towards his favourite preoccupations. This
change of outlook has naturally been accompanied by a
change in style and genre. It would have been difficult, on
the basis of his early naturalistic novels, to anticipate the
satirist and caricaturist who emerged with *The Incomparable Atuk* and *Cocksure*. Certainly, the earlier novels
have something of the satirists's scepticism towards the
pretensions of his characters and they are not wholly without elements of wit and ironic observation, especially *The
Apprenticeship of Duddy Kravitz*. Critics have also com-
mented upon Richler's ability to render minor characters
briefly and sharply, at his best as memorable "humours."
But this is true of many realistic novels which one would
not think of categorizing as satires. Occasional satirical
elements are utilized by most novelists. It is another matter
altogether to step from a dominant narrative mode of
realistic characterization, verisimilitude of action and
psychological plausibility to a dominant mode of conscious
caricature in characterization, purposeful implausibility
of action and fantasy in events. For a novelist to alter his
style and narrative mode so decisively, a deliberate change
in moral outlook must have occurred. Style is, after all,
a reflection of the tone and angle of vision. One of

the theses of this interpretation is that, philosophically, Richler has moved from a tentative Romanticism to a kind of Classicism. This, I believe, has important implications for his change in genres and in his attitudes to the cultural context within which his fictions take place.

In Richler's first novel, *The Acrobats*, we can already see most of the materials that recur in his later work: power, egoism, self-realization, struggle for survival, the conflict of generations and youthful rebelliousness, the need to escape from a confining environment, the sense of moral disillusionment and the fear of failure. The form of his first novel (and of all his naturalistic novels) is that most traditional of fictional structures: the attempted progress of the sensitive young man (endowed with some of the qualities, particularly a self-regarding sensitivity, conventionally attributed at least since the individualistic romanticism of the nineteenth century to the figure of the artist) in escaping the fetters of an inhibiting situation and in advancing towards a form of independence, realization of what he takes to be his inherent potentialities or worldly success and recognition. In other words Richler's theme is that of the attempted rise from rags to riches, on several moral and aesthetic levels. In literature, it is the aesthetic partner of the maximizing of one's power through the opportunities of the market or the syndrome of the "careers open to talent" which emerged after the French Revolution. Like the dynamic individualism of post-revolutionary Europe, it often operates through forms of symbolic parricide and regicide.

This configuration, of course, is not surprising in a novelist. It is a truism that the novel is *the* burgeois literary form. Theorists of the novel, like Ian Watt, have emphasized that the novel is specifically the literary form which is structured by the sense of time and movement as progressive, qualitative change, i.e. the notion that time must not be wasted and that the measurement of time should also measure changes in the person's status or situation. The novel is the form in which a person advances from A to B, and B is qualitatively different from A. Naturally it reflects a society where social mobility and the idea of self-development are both possible and social and psychological imperatives. The novel, therefore, is the form which best expresses romantic individualism (Hemingway pointed out, in *The Green Hills of Africa*, that Stendhal learned what the novel was about from Napoleon). Richler's novels are located in bourgeois time. His young men in a hurry or on the make (whether the hustler, Duddy Kravitz; the impatient aesthete, André Bennett; or the mixture of the two, Noah Adler) are the distant cousins, not only of Paul Morel, Stephen Dedalus and Sammy Glick, but also of Raskolnikov, Julien Sorel, Emma Bovary and Hedda Gabler. Like these nineteenth century heroes and heroines, they are manic depressive (the characteristic bourgeois psychosis, if we can believe the evidence of Ibsen and Flaubert). They urgently need to succeed and are haunted by the fear of failure; they alternate between delusions of triumph and a suicidal sense of utter emptiness.

Richler's novels differ, however, in that they are obviously of the middle of the twentieth century and lack much of the partial optimism current in the previous century. His characters are acutely aware that they come after the disillusionment with several twentieth-century revolutions and causes. If many of his figures appear to have the complacent resignation that is said to typify the decade of the 1950s (the setting of his first four novels), it is a resignation that is built on a sense of having been defeated. Up to a point, Hedda Gabler was confident she could manipulate life so that she would be able successfully to live in a condition of beauty and excitement. If we compare Richler's figures with even a defeated nineteenth century woman, we can readily see how much more resigned and defeated are Richler's mid-twentieth century figures. Richler's characters, for all their ambition and energy, really know *from the beginning* that either they are defeated or their outcomes will be much drearier than their apparent victories might indicate. Duddy Kravitz, for example, appears successful in achieving his ambition. But there is every indication that he has been metamorphosed into something very like his antagonist, the odious Jerry Dingleman.

A further problem for Richler's protagonists (and it is a problem, often, with the novels themselves) is that they do not know what it is they are seeking. Time and again, they comment that they know everything they are against and not what they are for. In some instances, they say they cannot even choose their enemies, for this implies which side they will take. They try, unsatisfactorily, to take a stand against choosing anything at all. They insist that salvation lies only in the adoption of personal values, but they are not sure which personal values to hold. The statement, in fact, becomes a mechanical formula with which they try to persuade themselves of something, rather than any passionately held and confident sense of personal identity. This becomes a problem for the reader as well as for the fictional character and represents the greatest weakness in Richler's writings. I don't mean to suggest that Richler ought to supply his characters with a facile affirmation. The problem is a genuine one. (This, I suppose, is why some people have referred to Richler's "existentialism." But this kind of comment, besides betraying a lack of understanding of existentialism as a philosophical standpoint, is itself a facile evasion of a problem and a retreat into a mechanistic formula.)

To be frank, it gets rather boring to be told repeatedly that all the good old causes are dead, that one knows what one dislikes but not what one likes, and then to be expected to be deeply concerned with the activities and fate of a very self-serving and self-pitying character. If he were simply an energetic, fun-loving "picaro," that might be all right. But since both the author and the fictional figure demand that the character be taken seriously as morally profound and probing, this just isn't good enough—especially several decades after Hemingway did this sort of thing pretty definitively.

For myself, I am always rather puzzled by critics (and there are many of them) who take at face value the moral posturings of many of Richler's main characters. After all, if we look at them with a cold eye, we often get a picture in which they appear something like this: they are egocentric and insensitive to others; they are ruthless and are basically indifferent even to those they sometimes claim to love; they will exploit or misuse their closest friends and relatives often on not much more than a whim; their claims to their own moral sensitivity and dilemmas are generally self-serving; they are usually contemptuous of the causes served by others at great personal risk; and they give little evidence of possessing either the kind of intelligence or knowledge which would be required to sustain the complexities and subtleties of the moral consciousness to which they pretend. Indeed, most of Richler's youthful rebels and idealistic questers share many characteristics with the hypocritical older generation, or the corrupt society, or the oppressors against whom they appear to be in revolt.

Although a number of examples could be cited, I will mention two that are particularly revealing of the self-willed and self-serving nature of the presumably idealistic questers. In *The Acrobats*, André Bennett rejects the revolutionary communism of his Spanish friend, Guillermo. He says he only admires ". . . the man who rises above the restrictions of his own class to assert himself as an individual and humanitarian." André, of course, feels a vague sense of discomfort in the presence of Guillermo. Although he says he believes himself in commitment to action and opposition to capitalism, he is embarrassed by his friend's real commitment to action at grave personal risk. Since he cannot be as cynical about Guillermo's political activism as he can be about the armchair radicals of the intelligentsia he recalls from his university days, he resorts to a crude and fashionable cocktail-party Nietzscheanism. It is particularly galling for this son of a wealthy Westmount family, who has the leisure and money to transcend the conventions of his class and to become a voyeur in the world of poverty and revolutionism, to accuse the poor of being concerned with injustice only because of their poverty and to scorn the proletariat for acting like a proletariat. He would prefer that they transcend their class limitations in order to search for some kind of inner illumination of being, as he, as an artist, hopes to do.

Similarly, in *Son of a Smaller Hero*, Noah Adler equates the domestic hypocrisies of the Goldenberg family (mainly their sexual repressions, for example Harvey not admitting he is a repressed homosexual) with the German people's refusal to recognize the existence of Nazi atrocities when the evidence was readily discernible. To say these acts are of the same quality, as Noah does, is simply stupid. It strongly belies Noah's claims to moral seriousness and sensitivity.

Despite these instances (of which there are many), Richler does make claims on the reader to view with sympathy and concern the problems of his heroes. As many critics have pointed out, the author is often emotionally engaged himself with his heroes. This clear call for sympathy with these figures, many of whom objectively have unsympathetic or dull personalities, has divided Richler's readers. There are those who find the novels almost wholly objectionable because of the repugnant qualities of so many of the characters. Others are taken in by the postures adopted by his sensitive or lonely young men and thus uncritically proceed to sentimentalize these figures as courageous knights who assault the unrelieved evil of a corrupt society —whether that society be composed of parlour radicals,

Hollywood entrepreneurs, sterile academics, capitalists or middle-class Jews in Montreal.

There is another possible approach to the reading of Richler's novels. One of the most interesting facts about these novels is that the ostensible heroes and the ostensible villains share many qualities. It is entirely possible to regard the apparent heroes unsympathetically and to respond even to the most malevolent figures, like the Nazi Kraus, Melech Adler, or Karp, sympathetically. Indeed, Richler's ability to make his characters sufficiently complex and humanly ambiguous, in a perfectly plausible manner, and to supply enough information so that we understand how they got to be the way they are is one of his most striking achievements. Some critics may fail to see the humanity in an apparently monstrous figure or naively may be taken in by a putatively sympathetic figure, but Richler the novelist does not make these mistakes.

Others have noted that Richler's characters are often "survivors" and that much of their energy is consumed by the strategies of survival in a competitive and hostile world. This is true enough. The Richler characters often have the wary, suspicious, necessarily egoistic psychology of the survivor. They move through life like tacticians, are survivors of concentration camps; various forms of persecution, war, or poverty; or simply painfully traumatic personal experiences and shattered dreams and ideals. They are frequently the floating debris of the wreckage of the modern period and this mental set conditions them to ruthlessness, emotional detachment and scepticism. Whatever hopes they have are tempered by an instinctive awareness of great odds against them. This often concludes in cynicism, barely suppressed hysteria, or submissive resignation.

A Choice of Enemies deals most explicitly with this kind of experience. The German refugee, Ernst, is Richler's archetype of the survivor. Richler employs this motif of the survivor to elicit the sense of shared experience and common problems among very different kinds of persons, even among antagonists. The radical exiles from Hollywood and Ernst heartily detest each other, but they are all survivors. Ernst was in the Hitler Youth and Karp was in a Nazi concentration camp, but they recognize a basic modern experience in each other. They have each been forced to abandon any vestige of honour in their respective struggles for survival. These ambivalent relationships in *A Choice of Enemies* can be seen as paradigms of many relationships in the other novels. In *The Acrobats*, for example, Kraus and André are deadly rivals. Kraus murders André. But the son of his mistress, Toni, is actually the son of Kraus. The baby is named André, but looks like Kraus. If the child is meant to be a symbolic reborn André (which is certainly the hope of Toni), he is also ironically the reborn Kraus. Kraus and André are brought together in a curious unity. Indeed, at one time André had a hallucination in which Kraus was striking old Mr. Blumberg, when it was André himself who had assaulted him. On another occasion, the figures of Blumberg and Kraus join as one in André's mind as a single symbol of his enemy. Thus, the semi-conscious associations of his mind unite him with the very figure of his antagonist. Moreover, Kraus and André, though politically as well as personally opposed, are actuated by images of what they ought to become which have been imposed upon them by others. Kraus is an apostle of fascism because he has been moulded this way by his manipulative sister. André is impelled by a romantic self-image induced in him by the intellectual fantasies of his mother and her circle. As much as André is sardonic about his mother (as Kraus is ambivalent about his sister), he is a product of her cultural milieu.

This leads us to a consideration which is at the heart of Richler's books. The figures of the romantic individualist and the survivor merge. But not only in the obvious sense that the survivor is perforce an isolated individual. What I am suggesting is that the very concept of the romantic quest of the individual hero, either for worldly success or for self-realization, is itself treated in Richler's novels as a part of the debris that lingers after a cultural wreckage. Although Richler's heroes, from André Bennett to Duddy Kravitz, embrace this romantic concept, the concept itself is no longer wholly intact for these characters. There is something inauthentic, even spurious, about the quality of their hopes and quests. It is intimately related to their sense that they know what they oppose, but not what they positively want. And it is the reason they cannot formulate their ambitions with any more precision than that. There is the sense with several of Richler's more important characters that they *must*, even involuntarily, engage in individualistic, quixotic quests—although they can't say why and are sceptical if any reasons are proffered. Ironically, the young Richler hero has a culturally induced instinct—almost a blind instinct—to be rebellious, individualistic, iconoclastic. He must revolt against an Establishment and its values, whether that establishment be represented by a paternal figure, a teacher or professor, a philistine capitalist or a religious fanatic. They know they don't like these things, but will quickly admit that they can't suggest anything that is necessarily better. Significantly, collective actions like socialism are also spurned, but a bit more respectfully. It has its appealingly rebellious side, but also its establishment in the Soviet Union. Above all, however, it belongs to the generation of their fathers and its collectivism inhibits the autonomy of the individualistic hero.

Characteristically, Richler's protagonists are those romantic, adolescent (of whatever age) "rebels without a cause" popularized by James Dean in the 1950s. This hero has no particular notions about the reconstruction of society or about the reconstruction of himself. His individualism is a matter of posture, a stance without content he adopts in opposition to his society. Hence, it is often expressed as a generational conflict between fathers (or grandfathers) and sons, as this is generally the most content-less of conflicts and the most readily articulated in terms of style of life—as only styles change drastically in a single generation. Basically, it is a rebellion enacted simply because one wants to adopt an attitude of rebellion; one wishes to irritate the "squares" of the establishment.

I don't mean to pretend that some of Richler's figures do not suffer genuinely at the hands of their parents or communities. In many cases they clearly do and they are sometimes authentically shocked or repelled by hypocrisies they encounter. But frequently the degree of their contempt seems unwarranted by the objective quality of the putative cause. Frequently, their rebellious stance precedes the existence of any solid reason for it and eagerly seeks out rationalizations after the fact. Noah Adler, like others, has just grievances. But he also feels a deep kinship with his grandfather (and despite his insistence on honesty, not least in their common capacity for cold egoism and ruthless cunning), and he admires much of his grandfather's religious tradition and discipline. Melech Adler is possibly the only person in his experience for whom he has an authentic admiration and respect, yet he revolts most immediately and passionately against him and everything he stands for. His revolt is primarily against the traditional social values of authority, obedience and duty in the abstract and is as much symbolic as actual. Melech's name, which means "king," underlines the elements of psychological parricide and regicide in Noah's actions. Similarly, Noah's father finds himself tempted once, in his role as a son to Melech, to murder the king and father. Throughout the novels there are many instances where a younger man voluntarily assumes the psychological role of son to an older man or woman and then turns against them. The older person is usually childless, but wants children, and seeks out surrogate children who will betray them. If the youthful Richler hero may be described as simply wanting to "do his thing," his thing often enough seems to be devouring his parent figures. The surrogate father figures, like Norman Price and Theo Hall, pay their nostalgic respects to their own vanished youth by willingly presenting themselves for the feast, masochistically re-enacting themselves in their surrogate children.

Clearly defined motives and desires do not exist in relation to these figures, even for Duddy Kravitz and his ambition to acquire land. Rather, there are threads of various possible motives, often mutually contradictory, in the same person: escape from poverty and weakness, a search for economic security, the vague need to define one's own identity, a desire for a form of ecstasy, and others. To put it another way, their motives are a mixture of the varieties of motives that can be isolated in the heroes and heroines of nineteenth century literature. They combine the motivations of Flaubert's Emma Bovary, Thackeray's Becky Sharp, and the Byronic hero. Even materialistic ambition can co-exist with, or be a kind of displacement of, a drive to exist on a plane of pure beauty; for example the music of Vivaldi which haunts Noah Adler. Even with Ernst and Duddy Kravitz, their material ambitions appear to be a tragic diversion from or displacement of basically aesthetic sensibilities. (This, sometimes, could even be said to be true of some of the hucksters, promoters, and exploiters in *The Incomparable Atuk* and *Cocksure*, where aesthetics have been subsumed by a world of status-hunting and commodity-marketing).

The repression and distortion of aesthetic values into their antitheses is one of the themes of Richler's writings. The more closely one examines the typical Richler character, the more evident it becomes that his actions are predicated on the idea of the expression of sensibility itself. It is not only the idea that the inner, private sensibility ought to remain inviolate (old Melech Adler, keeping the talismans of this sensibility locked in a secret strong box, provides a significantly ironical paradigm of this quality conventionally given to the young romantic hero). Richler's characters often aspire as well towards existing on a plane of pure, exquisite sensibility; a form of ecstasy. This, too, is in the Romantic tradition and is usually represented as the beatific side of the romantic individualist's medal. It is the reverse, yet the mirror image (Dorian Gray's mirror-portrait is the archetype of this paradoxical conjunction) of the individualist as robber baron or mercenary buccaneer.

Not infrequently, Richler's characters have something of the temperament of Henry James's Hyacinth Robinson in *The Princess Casamassima*; where Hyacinth's desire to be a small, but integral, part of an anarchist assassination plot is likened to existing in the aesthetic condition of a single musical note in an orchestral performance. Hyacinth wishes to exist in a state of disembodied ecstasy, for which he uses a musical metaphor. His motive is spiritual, although its enactment is material and the motive remains constant beneath the contradictions of his actual activities and choices. The motive is also psychological, as it is predicated on his deeply imprinted sense of personal depravity and unworthiness—a sense from which he wishes to be cleansed. Although sin, guilt and purification obviously have much lesser roles in Richler than in James, nevertheless they are not entirely absent. As early as André Bennett in *The Acrobats*, Richler has figures who are partly driven by a sense of guilt or the memory of a dishonourable past of which they would like to purge themselves. Their striving for autonomy and the kind of fresh start which might release them from past generations and traditions is related to this. (This process is satirized in *Cocksure*, where liberated "trendiness" is the new, post-romantic purification process, e.g. in Mortimer Griffin's wife, Joyce, or in the private school where the pupils mount theatrical productions after the inspiration of the Marquis de Sade.)

The apparently inconsistent and confused motivations, the intransigent negativism, the moral attitudinizing, and the nebulously inarticulate anti-authoritarianism of Richler's heroes can be resolved and made articulate by the idea of sensibility. The characters usually will themselves into the attitude of the neo-Byronic hero. Thumbing their noses at an Establishment becomes the main expression and content of their rebellion, an act more of gesture than of coherent substance. A curious determinism, in fact, has molded them into the style and expression of "free spirits." Psychologically and historically they are the consequences of the romantic cult of self-expression, long after the substance has been drained out of the concept and all that remains are the involuntary reflexes of the old romantic revolution. As Marx said of historical repetition, the first time is tragedy and the second time is farce. History weighs heavily, if unconsciously, on these youths. But it is a specific history which has run its course and has left them only with the possibility of compulsively mechanical gestures which once, perhaps, had meaning.

These youths, after all, are the inheritors of the propaganda of the romantic era. Their imaginations have been nourished by the contemporary packaged versions of the dreams of that era: Byronism filtered through Hollywood films, the legends of heroically successful self-made men, and unreal images of a war in Spain ironically made seductively exotic through the songs of the losing side. In the synthetic myths of their popular culture, objective disparities and contradictions merge into a unitary image of glamour where capitalism's rugged individualist and the itinerant revolutionist present a single model to be imitated. Sensing also that this image presents a false model of reality, they nonetheless are fired by the romance they feel it ought to mirror. This accounts for their own mimicry of a posture they know to be anachronistic and their

deep resentment of that history and those older generations which foisted such a dream upon them.

In *Son of a Smaller Hero* Aaron Panofsky is sullenly
resentful towards his communist father who inspired him
to enlist in the Spanish Civil War where he lost his legs.
It is one of the relatively minor father-son relationships in
Richler's work, but recalling it reveals much about the
nature of generational conflict in these novels and illumi-
nates how pervasive is this quality in these books. It is
also true that the older generation in Richler's work (the
Theo Halls and Norman Prices) have been sons to other
fathers and have also been inspired and victimized by
similar visions. This links the dilemmas of fathers and sons
in an intergenerational iron chain of determinism where,
with considerable irony, they are almost mechanically
programmed to re-enact the ceremonies of "free spirits.'

It is for this reason (although the process began in *A
Choice of Enemies*) that in *Atuk* and *Cocksure* the most
contemptuous satire is reserved for the information media
—the world of film, TV, advertising, journalism and publishing—the pop culture industries which manipulate
dreams and visions, determine the sensibilities of the popu-
lace, tamper with souls en masse. Star Maker (radically
complete unto himself, the consummation of Romanticism), in *Cocksure*, is thus far Richler's most remarkably
concentrated symbol for the destructively manipulative
force of a spent historical romanticism. Combining nar-
cissism and cannibalism (like Atuk and others in the book
of that name) and fusing the images of the mass media
manipulator and the father figure, the childless Star
Maker dismembers and devours his adoptive children.
But at the same time he inspires his mass audiences of
Duddy Kravitzes and Noah Adlers to aspire to the image
of "stars," simultaneously on the planes of material power
and romantic sensibility. The acolytes of the celestial Star
Maker are the figurative descendants of Duddy Kravitz.

There is only so far an author can go with a historical and cultural situation which is trapped in a dead-end sensibility of burnt-out romanticism where the sensitive young men of the bourgeois epoch are fated to acting out illusions they can no longer believe. This, of course, is one of the fundamental problems of the novel today. The fact that the novel developed while formulating the ideology of that epoch is an important reason why so many contemporary novels are reduced to synthetically frenetic repetitions of the ethos of *Huckleberry Finn*. It is as if frenzied overstatement could resurrect the culturally dead the way Baroque art sought to restore the late medieval ethos through exaggeration of expression. An approach to Richler's writings like that of his earlier commentator Warren Tallman, who fundamentally misreads the import and direction of these novels, only sentimentalizes the hybrid Faustianism of a Duddy Kravitz. Reading through American ideological glasses, he sees Richler's themes as variants of the antihistorical innocence of American frontier ideology and manifest destiny at the very moment when Richler is beginning to satirize this romantic Faustianism almost as lucidly as Conrad does in *Heart of Darkness*. Such an approach cannot account for Richler's tactical shift from involvement to detachment and his adoption of satire as a formal mode (as opposed to satirical flashes in basically naturalistic novels) while maintaining his hold on the same set of cultural materials as subject matter.

After his first four novels, it would appear that Richler clearly realized a need to get away from characters attempting to live according to the measurements of bourgeois time, i.e. the belief that one could go from A to B, and that B represented progress compared to A. As it was, his characters had strong doubts that such movement was possible or significant even though they tried it. Comic forms, including satire, present one way out of this situation. In satires like *Atuk* and *Cocksure* we are no longer in the world of progressive and incremental mobility, even though men and women on the make still inhabit the world of these books. But the focus of interest here is no longer on their progress. We are not especially interested whether or not they achieve their purported goals and we are aware that it is not significant whether or not they do. This particular shaping of our responses is assured because the author presents his characters as self-evident stereotypes. As soon as we see them, we know what they are like without waiting for their stories to unfold. We recognize them as caricatures of familiar attitudes and behaviour patterns, largely caricatures representing aspects of the world of contemporary popular culture. Significant time in these satires works something like a palimpsest. It is not so much that the characters are living in time, but rather that time is simply a device whereby the reader gains more knowledge. The fictional time is relatively static as the characters do not grow and change. Rather, the reader simply sees layers being peeled away which reveal to him more information about the nature and meaning of the relationships and encounters among the various patterns of conduct of which the characters are emblems. The reader's response, therefore, is more cerebral than emotional. The satirical mode is closer to the purely intellectual.

One cannot, of course, assume that Richler will choose always to write in the same vein. As his perceptions of his materials change, so will his fictional techniques. But in these two latest books, he has begun to write comedy of manners and has revealed a spirit far closer to that of Congreve, Swift, and Shaw than one might have guessed from his earlier novels. He is certainly a long way from the spirit of Caliban which Warren Tallman (after Leslie Fiedler) sees as characteristic of American writing and in which tradition Tallman perversely wishes to place him. As much as it might disturb some, Richler has begun to show something of Prospero's sceptical magic.

In my view, there is frequently an element of nihilism in the literary genre of comedy, particularly in its satirical side. I do not want to exaggerate this, but I think there is a nihilistic trace that is an inevitable derivative of the conservative nature of comedy even in that form of comedy (which is not Richler's form, anyway) that ends happily with a ritualized sense of renewal. These elements of renewal and nihilism co-exist in a complex and fascinating tension. There is something about comedy that is not open-ended; that inflexibly closes off possibilities and is antipathetic to the idea of growth and change. It is not a form beloved by romantics and most of the great comic artists of English literature have not been romantics. In comedy, a specific form of social organization is being preserved and some representations of alternative ways of being are exorcised. But to attempt to preserve an organism without allowing for change and growth, paradoxically without allowing the organism to negate itself, is an endeavour which does have a touch of nihilism. I am not suggesting this as pejorative in terms of literary quality. Some of the finest literature has this dimension. The art of James Joyce (which constitutes the most powerful critique of romanticism and the principle of generative growth in modern literature) has this quality. This is why the solemn D. H. Lawrence hated Joyce's work so much.

An artist formulates and articulates the complex interactions of cultural experience. He does not prescribe for it. Richler makes no attempt at being a philosopher of history or a social visionary. Like many modern writers, he is aware that we are still wrestling with the problems bequeathed to us from the nineteenth century—that, indeed, twentieth century man is still intellectually and emotionally parasitic upon the concepts and dreams that both flourished and began to dissolve in the previous century. We still live with specific historical ghosts. The Romantic Revolution may be over, but its Faustianism is still operative in a thousand posthumous ways. Richler has no facile answers for this cultural situation and he eschews the posturings of prophecy. Proponents of a brave new world do not write comedies of manners. He is a writer devoted to his craft and the purpose of his craft is to articulate experience as it truly is. The immediate task of his craft is to discover fictional strategies for the accurate representation of reality. To represent the current dilemmas of the legacy of romanticism in the cold light of comedy is an illumination we require.

London, England
August 1970

G. DAVID SHEPS

AND THE SUN GOES DOWN
Richler's First Novel

GEORGE BOWERING

*One generation passeth away, and another generation
cometh: but the earth abideth for ever*

In Mordecai Richler's first novel there is a Jewish American businessman who has changed his name from Lazarus
to Larkin. That leaves no Lazarus to be raised from the
dead; he will go about the process of mouldering along
with nearly everyone else he meets in America and Valencia, the sad worn-out sacrificial portion of Spain, Europe
and the world that is the setting for *The Acrobats*.

In 1957 an interview with Richler appeared in the
Tamarack Review in which he referred to people "living
in a time . . . when there is no agreement on values . . .
there has been a collapse of absolute values, whether that
value was Marx or God or Gold [all three treated discon-
solately in the novel]. We are living in a time when superficially life seems meaningless, and we have to make value
judgements all the time, it seems in relation to nothing,"
Richler is here talking about his problem, and the problem of André Bennett, the young Canadian painter-
acrobat adrift in the city of Valencia during fiesta time,
April 1951, a decade and a half after the bell tolled for
Robert Jordan, alone and dying on a mountain trail soon
to be trod by Franco's fascists.

André sits at the café tables in the Lost Generation of
his mind, stuck behind the wrong World War that he was
too young to enter or understand, "so he came to Spain—

From *Canadian Literature*, No. 29 (Summer 1966); pp. 7-17. By permission of the author.

Valencia, where the killing had started in a way and maybe they could explain it." But Ernest Hemingway is not there; neither is the Spain of Hemingway's books. Through the work of Hemingway, from the beginnings in the first short stories to *The Old Man and the Sea*, there is a growing sense of commitment, not necessarily of man to cause, but of man to men. This is the painfully learned realization of the constantly aging Hemingway hero, that as the world of the twentieth century becomes more huge in its antihuman machinery, the people under the machines must reach out more generously to one another. "No man is an island" is the motto set to Hemingway's novel of the Spanish war, where the members of the Lost Generation find at least each other under the bombs of the twentieth century's least human machine—Fascism. In 1951 Spain Richler's anti-hero demonstrates the disappointment in the notion that such a painfully made commitment was to be invalidated by the ensuing victory of the World War and the subsequent transformation of men to smaller machines, servants to the master robot.

In fact Richler sometimes seems to sacrifice his art to a love-hate attitude to Hemingway's works, especially to *For Whom the Bell Tolls*. In the beginning of *The Acrobats* there is a noticeable Hemingway influence, in the artificial dialogue, in the sentence order and length:

In the summer they would take us out in the boats, and we would jump overboard and swim. The water was very cool, and there was always the taste of salt in our mouths. The priests said it was evil because we all swam and played together and we were often naked. My father laughed at the priests. He said they had filthy minds. At night there was always dancing on the quays, especially when there was a good catch. That night there was only the noise of the shooting.

Sometimes André Bennett thinks, perhaps consciously, as if he were Frederic Henry:

Love, he thought. That is one of the words that is no longer any good. *Like courage, soul, beautiful, honour,* and so many others. Words that have become almost obscene because of hack writers.

Doubly sad for André, because at least Frederic Henry had a world war to blame. It is not only Richler who has Hemingway on the mind. At least part of the time André's resentment, his feeling of being trapped in the wrong disillusioning time, is turned against Hemingway's Spanish experience:

"As a matter of fact," André said, "I'm not really a painter at all. I came here to study life in its entirety. One day I hope to write a book about it. You know, like that *Who do the Bells Toll For.*"

But this is Richler's first book, and as often happens in first books, the young author's literary ghosts are difficult to allay. So that later, when André is preparing in his drunkenness to poke his fist at the Nazi Kraus, Richler sees him through the literary trick (Hemingway's word) that comes via Hemingway's "Up in Michigan" from the advice of Gertrude Stein:

André laughed. He laughed and laughed and laughed. He laughed because Chaim was a useful man and he laughed because Kraus was a brute. He clutched the banister and doubled up laughing. He laughed because Ida was dead and he laughed because probably he did not love Toni. He laughed because he was drunk. He laughed and laughed. He laughed because he was feverish and he laughed because the doctors said he would go mad. Tears rolled down his cheeks, and he laughed.

All the directionless bar scenes of *The Acrobats* are like expatriate *The Sun Also Rises* scenes, but without even the desperate gaiety of the Jake Barnes crowd—rather with a soft and aimless self-hate. When André is invited into a tryst with Jessie, the wife of sad American tourist Larkin, he goes along, saying only, "Okay, I guess," and again, "Okay." Later, when Jessie tries to get his clothes off in the hotel room, he simply mopes around till her embarrassing husband appears, and it is too late.

The acrobats of the novel are also sad clowns, wearing sad faces under their sad faces of make-up. The world is a big-top where the same tired music grinds every day, and the variety act appears monotonously every afternoon, every night. In Valencia it is festival time, the loud drunken blaze of colour and fire that comes every year to use up whatever small flames may still lick in the bellies of the citizens, inheritors of the worn earth tramped for centuries by armies of Araby, France, the Vatican and, latterly, Franco and now the also defeated foreigners from two continents.

In Richler's eyes the place where the killing began is still an ugly disaster area, where the centuries-shattered survivors pick their way among the rubble of each other. The wanderings of the foreigners take place among constant images of beggars, cripples, forced prostitutes taken by police for protection, not only the war-blighted of Spain, but of this focus of Europe and the world. This is the post-Hemingway world, the post-*For Whom the Bell Tolls* world, where the sermon from Donne takes on a grim cast. The language of Richler and his characters is also post-Hemingway, with all rapture gone, all romanticism sifted out. The (anti)hero's girl is not brave Maria in a sleeping bag, but the pregnant prostitute Toni, not the rebellious Pilar of the mountains but the city-slum girl tired of revolution and war, who can say of Spain only:

—pooh! There has always been poverty. You can do nothing, do you understand? Nothing! Why? Wh— What is the use of talking? Kill and kill and kill. Me, I would rather live on my knees. Now I have said it!

Almost all the people in the novel are tired and disappointed. André is a man in his twenties, a young artist, with little responsibility, but his disappointment is the largest. It is enough to bring him to his own miserable end. His disappointment is the largest, and the least understandable—it is a kind of symbolic disappointment, where the figure of the man stands head-bowed between the stories of the prewar West, and the actual bomb-broken buildings of 1951.

The young artist's opposite number is the ex-Olympic athlete Reinhold Kraus, the Nazi for whom the present Spain is another kind of disappointment. Fascism is not the success it had seemed to be after the Civil War, in which Kraus had been Hitler's man there. Now the country is lax, disorderly, Semitic, effeminate, undermined by the Communist underground.

In the triangle of André-Toni-Kraus there is a kind of allegory. In many instances Toni, the postwar girl of the bars and streets, speaks for war-weary Spain, expressing the desire to get out of the ideological war, and seeking means to survive. When André says that he is in Spain to find out what mid-century is all about, he knows that his attempts to make a loving relationship with Toni are infibulated by the guilt he carries about the abortion death of the Jewish girl he had slept with in his college-Montreal recent past. For Kraus, Toni is important because she is carrying his child. At one point Kraus is seen writing in his diary, linking in his thoughts the rebirth of Nazism and the child of infiltration in Toni's womb. Eventually the two rivals meet on a bridge over the tired Spanish river, and worn-out old athlete kills worn-out young artist and a group of impoverished postwar citizens descends on the loser, stripping him of his raiment and hiding the naked body in a cave.

Barney Larkin is the disappointed Jewish American tourist, who began as a poor boy, got rich in a kind of mid-century American dream, and has now found out that riches have not made him charming and sought-after, especially not by his wife, Jessie. Jessie, a Gentile, married Barney (Lazarus) Larkin for his money and, in her disappointment, finds that money cannot buy back her time, or his virility.

Brooding behind all the personal disappointments is the failure of the social revolution, the shock that came with the victory of tyranny and poverty. Though some revolutionaries like Guillermo still wander about Spain, in and out of Valencia, and André's life, they are bitter, as if regretting the failure of the revolution, not looking forward to its coming. Pepe and María are seen at times in the novel. Pepe, the poor husband out of work, has seen the failure of the revolution, has still the simple faith to admire André's paintings—he has not been entirely embittered by the failure. He is married to the Catholic María, who is at last pregnant after many disappointments. Pepe is a nickname for José, so they are Joseph and Mary, an example of Richler's early obvious attempts at symbolism. But Pepe is cynical about the chances for the child of Joseph and Mary:

. . . Why should I be pleased. . . . If he is any good, they will get him like they got the others. And if he is going to be bad I do not want him.

In *A Farewell to Arms*, those who oppose their humanity to the great machines of gods and men perish young. In *The Acrobats*, those characters who try to struggle for a cause that is perishing or is hiding within them, die (André, Guillermo), while the ones who accept defeat and disillusionment live on and pass to new times and places (Chaim, the wise and hounded Jew; Juanito, the gentleman turned pimp; Derek, the Civil War Republican poet become dissolute alcoholic and homosexual).

Pretty obviously Richler intends in this first novel to show his own disillusionment in a postwar world he never made nor even had a hand in destroying. The form of the story shows that. While André Bennett, self-exiled young Canadian artist in Spain, is the character with whom the author most closely identifies, *The Acrobats* is not his story alone. The book is made up of shuffled scenes, the searching spotlights shift from acrobat to acrobat, lighting now Barney in his frightened New World foray into a blunt Spanish whorehouse, now André lying in his rat-infested room beside an unfinished painting of woe, now Kraus in his Nazi sex-problem, unable to cope with women or intellect. The lights probe all over Valencia in the present, but also into the past of Montreal and Madrid and Businesstown, U.S.A. The different people cross each other in different places, the whole acrobatic routine, and snippets of knowledge are exchanged with handholds. We watch not the performance of one man's life, but the tumbling pattern of the human condition. Each player hides his own version of guilt, secret from the rest. The recent past in each case haunts the present, and promises no good future —for any of the characters of the novel, for Spain, for mid-century World. Doggedly, the Valencians burn their traditional exorcistic *fallas*, and Derek says of that futile diversion:

Perhaps in all of us there is some evil, and we're just too weak to burn it. So we build evil toys and dance around them. Later we burn them, hoping, perhaps, that it will help.

But still we return to André. He is not the centre of the world, but his disillusionment and failure are special, of a particular kind. He is the only character whose experience does not include the war of the Thirties and Forties, except in the way he remembers, the child's participation in wartime mottos and propaganda formulas. If somehow Toni represents Spain, André represents the postwar consciousness of the West.

Chaim, the Jewish bar-owner, is a kind of wandering Jew and, like Jung's wise old man, he offers the wisest words on André's problem. Chaim has been hounded from country to country, various ideologies at his heels, and fully understands that no "cause" holds the promise for (a) man's salvation. It is curious to note that his name may be a pun. Mahavira, the founder of Jainism, said, "Within yourself lies salvation." Chaim, the founder of Chaimism, says, "But there is no cause that saves us all. Salvation is personal."

André realizes the hopelessness of the war-fraught twentieth-century causes:

Often it appeared to André that he belonged to the last generation of men. A generation not lost and not unfound but sought after zealously, sought after so that it might stand up and be counted, perjuring itself and humanity, sought after by the propagandists of a faltering revolution and the rear guard of a dying civilization. His intellectual leaders had proven either duds or counterfeits—standing up in the thirties to cheer the revolution hoarsely, and in the fifties sitting down again to write a shy, tinny, blushing yes to capitalistic democracy.

Nobody could quite believe again that he had grown up to find all gods dead, all wars fought, all faiths in men shaken. There was going to be another war all right—their war. The old gods, newly cleaned and pressed, were being gleefully handed down to them.

But he is, despite his sophistication, a production of the middle of the twentieth century, and the inheritor of its debts. Chaim, a man who seems to have seen all generations, knows, that, "The fun will be for André's and Toni's generation. They will have to pay the unpaid bills of the past, account for the dishonesties, the vagrancies. . . ." But Chaim knows also (as André seems not to) that there is always a time after the wars; and now that it is fifteen years after the Spanish war, and six years after the World War, it is time to quit looking over one's shoulder:

It is that he knows and understands all the things that he is against but he still doesn't know what he is *for*. André has the temperament of a priest, but none of the present churches will do. That makes it very difficult.

André, walking around Valencia, the scene of dogged celebration of the past, the ancient peoples of Spain, is also haunted by his own past, his share, perhaps, of a world guilt. There is an implied connection between Kraus's Nazi past and the guilt carried by André—he made a Montreal Jewish girl pregnant, and she died after her abortion; and when André went to see her family, the father told him to go away and leave them alone, ethnically. André hit the old man, knocking him down, carrying away with him that added guilt. At the point when he finishes telling this story to Toni, he finds himself looking into the Nazi eyes of Kraus. Now the dead girl stands or lies always between André and Toni. (As Nazi Kraus stands in the shadows, watching them.) Toni, the traditional prostitute looking for love, knows that André's ability to love is smothered by guilt:

And she felt fear, because she loved him with a hopeless beautiful love, knowing—always knowing—that he could not love, that something ugly and bitter within him would always stifle any love he felt for her.

And it is André's inability to love that is his grief and failure, because an inability to love is an inability to believe. Guillermo, his Communist friend, refuses to believe that André's salvation is personal:

"I remember when you were ill," he said, "when all you knew was despair, and all you did was drink. Do you know why, André? Not because of the girl and her father. That is only incidental. It is because you are without hope or reason or direction. You are *sin céntimo*. If you are a humanist there is only one place for you. You must join us."

André has at least the self-knowledge required to refute Guillermo's solution. But that leaves him looking into a void:

I guess my crime is that I haven't chosen, he thought. I wonder what my punishment will be. And who will be my judge?

Further, he knows that which Chaim suggests:

It is the man who is unusual—the man who rises above the restrictions of his own class to assert himself as an individual and humanitarian. It's pretty damn elementary to be aware of social injustice and poetic truth and beauty, but to be capable of empathy, to understand the failings of a man—any man—even as you condemn him, well— Look, every human being is to be approached with a sense of wonder. The rest is crap, or incidental.

Empathy—the quality of being able to feel another's joy or woe; André knows that his great sin is in not being committed to anyone outside himself. He still hears the old man saying leave us alone. But André is not in love with himself. In fact he seeks his own destruction. He is disgusted by his own failure of commitment—it is with disgust towards his own failure that he allows himself to say to Guillermo, "Everything is a joke. It has to be." And he feels uneasy before his father-figure when Chaim asks him what postwar youth believes in, and he replies with the facile formula, "I guess more than anything else we believe in not believing."

However, André is more interesting than that. At least his is an odyssey, slow-moving as it may be. He is looking for a grail without knowing what a grail is. We see him trying to make some act of commitment, even if it is an unsavory sexual one with Barney Larkin's wife, or a shameful drunken one in which he fecklessly punches Kraus and gets beaten up by that reluctant destroyer.

Chaim at one point recognizes that, in his wish to be committed, André carries at least the potentiality of his salvation. In fact, at one point, Chaim speaks perhaps like an indulgent father who does not care to discourage his son:

But I like you, André, because you are not bored. You are not intellectual and uncommitted. You are always taking part, even if not always intelligently. The earth is in your hands and you are dirty.

It is not the truth, of course, but it is a recognition of André's predilection toward goodness.

But in his search André gets lugubriously drunk, glamorizes his situation somewhat by calling his drunkenness madness, and walks through the Valencia streets of sordid escape. On his way towards whatever he is approaching, he hears a drab and drunken hopeless Spanish song of patriotism, love and religious faith:

> *Por mi patria y por mi novia*
> *y mi Virgen de San Gil*
> *y mi rosario de cuentas*
> *yo me quisiera morir.*

—traditionally honourable things to die for (and we know by now that André is on his way to dying), but all three things already dead inside André. In his pocket he has a thick wad of Chaim's money, money that promises to buy them escape, freedom in Paris, but he meets a mad whore and throws the wealth on her bare belly, feeling a mysterious release as he does. This is one of the best realized scenes in the novel, largely because it is one of the few that cannot be well interpreted or understood, because the manipulating intellect of the author is not obvious; it is like most good parts of a novel—only the feelings respond, the wish to intervene, the shock of sympathy for Chaim, whose chances seem to flutter to the floor with his Spanish money.

At the same time, we see André's growing haze of what he feels is insanity, and it wars for his mind against his desperation to be committed to anything, as long as the man can make an act, a gesture that is not escape or evasion. Once again it is confrontation with Kraus that seems to give him that chance. And once again Kraus pummels his antagonist, finally picks him up and hurls him off the bridge they meet on. André lies smashed on the rocks below and, in his last conscious thoughts, is trying to be committed at least to his own death:

He felt a lump in his throat but only dimly, as consciousness was slipping from him. He was sobbing. *No. No. All I ask is that I know what's going on. That's all. Never mind the cigarette. Just knowing. Or feeling.*

But at the moment that Kraus threw André from the bridge, the big final *falla* was exploding, so that we are reminded that André's way out is as much an evasion and a mollification as the Spanish indigent's yearly dazzlement.

Some critics have pointed out (and correctly, to a certain extent) that the people we meet in *The Acrobats* are stock characters. André is the young athlete, lost and in exile, searching for meaning in a confused world. Toni is the innocent prostitute, the traditional wry comment on a whole society that has sold its innocence for quick, mortal and illusory rewards. Chaim is the perennial wise old wandering Jew and father figure to those who have lost all their own fathers. Barney is the rich boorish American abroad, hiding secret fears of his own sexual inability behind an aggressive social manner. And so on.

Probably more to the point is that in this first novel, Richler has not yet, as he has in his later books, submerged the techniques of writing below the surface of the story as we are allowed a look at it. A reader notices this in the first few pages, in which André is introduced to the Americans. The scene-setting conversations around the sidewalk tables of Valencia are filled with obvious attempts to show that the writer is not simply reporting dialogue. Someone says something; then someone lights a cigarette; then someone says something. Or:

Derek lit a cigarette. He tossed his head back with studied abandon and blew a big puff of smoke into the still air. I shouldn't have come back, he thought. It was wrong.

Or "Jessie smiled brightly," then said something. "Jessie puckered up her cherry lips impatiently," then said something. "Jessie applauded," then said something.

On the other hand, or perhaps still with the too-obtrusive first hand, when Richler attempts some impressionistic writing, he is usually clumsy. An exception is in the scene of André's death, but this may be because few people are prepared to offer their knowledge in criticism of an experience they have not come away from yet. But when Richler offers an "impressionistic" picture of the festival streets, his plan is so obvious as to render the familiar techniques inadequate to the goal, the pen of the writer scratching in the ear.

Much more authentic and accomplished are the lyrical catalogues, of André's childhood experiences, of the political evils of mid-century, or of the sordid Valencia streets. Once Jessie loses her way in the backstreets of the Valencia markets, where:

The heat was redolent of rancid food, children with soiled underwear, uncovered garbage, venereal diseases, sweat and boils, pimpled adolescents with one leg and a stump for another, remedies exchanged across washing lines, cheats, cross-eyed whores, dirty persons, and no privacy.

Richler has a very good reporter's eye, and an equally good ear, especially for the individual rhythms and accents of speech. The wise, kindly, ironic Chaim is very well realized—Richler's best moments come when he gets Chaim's speech down, or the dialogue of any of his characters, American or Spanish, Nazi or Jew. Conversely, he is weakest, usually, when he goes after interior monologue; there he tends to go maudlin or hokey, sometimes unconvincingly clichéd.

Another point for Richler is his ability to take a basically negative character and to draw a sympathetic picture of him, as of the bourgeois Barney. This is a feat that Arthur Koestler rightly said should be accomplished by the good novelist. Critics will say, and have said, that Richler's characters are portrayed to be "undeserving of compassion" (Nathan Cohen in the *Tamarack Review*, Winter 1958), but I believe that the young Richler scored a coup in this novel, in arousing compassion for characters who would superficially seem to be the enemy—Barney and Kraus the best examples. In this way, Richler speaks not to the smug liberal intelligence, but to the compassionate human being who may be lurking behind that mask. No author who speaks that way can hope to write an "accomplished" novel. But the book reaches at least determinedly beyond accomplishment toward the place where a man is forced to ask himself where he is, and how he feels. And there the sun also rises again.

SON OF A SMALLER HERO

GEORGE WOODCOCK

"The ghetto of Montreal has no real walls and no true dimensions," says Mordecai Richler. "The walls are the habit of atavism and the dimensions are an illusion. But the ghetto exists all the same."

Son of a Smaller Hero is, in its narrowest sense, the account of an attempt by a Jewish youth in Montreal to escape from the mental bonds of the ghetto and, having passed through the feared and desired world of the *Goyim*, to realize his true self in the freedom which he believes exists beyond the invisible walls. Turning by turning, the vistas open. The little border territory in which Noah Adler's experiences are developed becomes the microcosm of a whole city, and, by the multiplication of reflections, the microcosm of a whole country that lives by the mutual attractions of the divided.

Son of a Smaller Hero is Mordecai Richler's second novel, published in 1955. It was preceded and followed by novels of modern Europe—*The Acrobats* (1954) and *A Choice of Enemies* (1957); in his fourth novel, *The Apprenticeship of Duddy Kravitz* (1959), Richler returned to the Jewish streets. In every way, but particularly in their control of the sensationalism that at its best gives vitality to his writing and at worst makes it banal, the Montreal novels are the best; with a small number of short stories dealing with people in the same environment, they form the body of work that made Richler, before he reached the age of thirty, the most important of the younger generation of Canadian fiction writers.

The particular success of novels like *Son of a Smaller Hero* and *The Apprenticeship of Duddy Kravitz* does not

---

The introduction to *Son of a Smaller Hero*; New Canadian Library, McClelland & Stewart Ltd., Toronto, 1966. By permission of McClelland & Stewart.

spring merely from the fact that Richler is understandably strongest when he stands on his own native ground and writes about the streets and the people that made up the environment of his youth. His success is also related to a phenomenon of which we have become increasingly conscious during the past decade—the fact that, as Roy Daniells pointed out recently in *Canadian Literature*, "the Jewish contribution to Canadian literature continues to be out of all proportion to the size of the Jewish element in our population." It is not merely a question of the quantity or even the remarkable quality of the Jewish contribution. Jewish writers have also revealed with peculiar force and sensitivity the tensions that are characteristic of Canadian life, and particularly of Canadian urban life. This, it seems evident, is because the themes of which they treat with such a complex heritage of experience, the themes of isolation and division, are also the themes from which it is difficult for any writer in Canada to escape. It might be a metaphorical exaggeration to describe Canada as a land of invisible ghettos, but certainly it is, both historically and geographically, a country of minorities that have never achieved assimilation.

It is this fact that makes Montreal a great frontier city, where various traditions intermingle and react upon each other. It is a natural laboratory for examining the fears and fascinations that flow between the various communities, and Richler, working outward from the Jewish environment of his own childhood, has presented us with such an examination in *Son of a Smaller Hero*. Yet *Son of a Smaller Hero* is not a sociologically slanted novel about the "problem" of Jewish-Gentile relationships like Gwethalyn Graham's *Earth and High Heaven*. Nor does Richler seek didactically to present us with lessons on the need for unity among Canadians, as Hugh MacLennan did in *Two Solitudes*. He does not, of course, ignore the social problems, yet at the same time he does not seek to abstract them from their context. They are part of the world he is trying to present in a fictionally viable form, part of the particular world of a divided city that he is using to illuminate a universal theme: the predicament of the man who sets out honestly to find and to be himself in a world where most men fear their own natures and try to live by comfortable falsehoods.

As most travellers know from experience, when different cultures meet, it is usually along their fraying edges that the least typical and often the most sensitive of their inhabitants are to be found. This is the case in *Son of a Smaller Hero*; it is Noah, the grandson of the Adler family, in rebellion against the wilful blindness by which his own relatives attempt to preserve their ghetto isolation, who becomes most deeply involved in the other world of the *Goyim*, and this involvement in its turn is consummated through his love affair with Miriam, a woman of French Canadian extraction who, after a tragic childhood, had sought refuge in that desert of the mind where academic hollow men, like her husband Theodore, pursue scholarship to compensate for their inadequacies as persons and as creative artists.

For Miriam the affair, which promises so much, is in the end destructive. Her neurotic desire for security wears away Noah's passion, which is not proof against the competing loyalties called back to life by the death of his father and the sickness of his mother. She returns, a stage nearer the final break-up, to the world from which she had hoped to escape.

Even for Noah the affair with Miriam is less intrinsically important than the space it takes up in the novel might at first sight lead one to assume. In the final pages of *Son of a Smaller Hero*, when Noah is about to leave for Europe— a decision that marks the second and final break with his past—it is no longer of Miriam that he thinks. The guilt over his desertion of her has quickly burnt out, for there is a strain of ruthlessness in Noah which in a later novel will be extravagantly magnified in the character of Duddy Kravitz. It is the difficult parting with his possessive mother, and, even more, the hope of reconciliation with

his domineering old grandfather, Melech Adler, that in
the end occupy his mind. Miriam, in fact, has been only
the centre of a catalytic incident in the difficult process of
understanding his environment, and thereby understanding and liberating himself, which for the reader begins
when Noah leaves home on the first page of the book to
live in a furnished room on Dorchester Street and ends
when he sails for Europe.

It is in the ghetto itself and in the Adler family that we
must seek the substance of Noah's struggle. This fact
Richler reveals to us not merely in the complexities of his
plot, but also in the differing ways in which he has presented the two worlds of *Son of a Smaller Hero*. The half-
Bohemian Gentile world from which Miriam emerges to
meet Noah is painted in greyish tones and blurred forms,
as befits a limbo of atrophied love and intellectual barren-
ness. The Jewish world is painted with a vivid impasto
which suggests the vitality and variety of human impulse
that stir beneath a surface stiffened by traditions and fears.
The background is rendered in a fine chiaroscuro in
which social darkness is illuminated by great flashes of
comedy; it erupts magnificently into the centre of the
picture in the mass hysteria that accompanies the funeral
of Noah's father, Wolf Adler, when he is mistakenly re-
garded as a hero who gave his life to save the rolls of the
Torah. The inhabitants of the ghetto are depicted with a
Dickensian eye for the foibles and tics of behaviour and
speech; this makes them memorable, but too often we remember the habitual behaviour rather than the person,
and Richler, in *Son of a Smaller Hero* at least, is inclined
to present his minor figures as humours rather than characters. His sense of satire leads him perilously near the
edge of caricature.

Yet the leaning towards caricature and its accompany-
ing savagery never outweighs the growing compassion that
accompanies Noah's understanding of his own world. In
that process Wolf Adler's death is the central incident
which exposes the whole pattern of private rebellion that

has spread its roots through the life of the Adler family. Wolf, working in the family scrap yard under old Melech's patriarchal tyranny, has been fascinated for years by the box that his father—Noah's grandfather—keeps in the safe and will only open when he has locked his office door. When Shloime, Melech's youngest son, rebels into minor gangsterism and sets fire to the scrap yard, Wolf's obsession leads him to run blindly into the burning office. Noah eventually finds him under the charred rubbish, with his dead hand inside the box; it contains no money, but it does contain the clues that will lead Noah eventually towards an understanding of his own world and his own nature.

The revelation, like the contents of the box, is of two kinds. When the onlookers see the sacred scrolls that lie on top, they raise the cry, "Wolf Adler gave his life for the Torah," and the man who died in a suicidal craving for money becomes a saint of the ghetto. To his horror, Noah sees that even those of his relatives who do not believe the legend are ready to support it for their own advantage.

Thus the box creates a lie, but it also reveals a truth when Noah examines the bundle of photographs and letters he has found there and concealed in his own pocket. As he rather guiltily looks through them, his life is suddenly filled with echoes; he realizes that, just as he sought liberation through his affair with Miriam, so, forty years before, his orthodox grandfather carried on a love affair with a Gentile girl in Europe, and even continued until his old age to write her letters that were never posted. He also finds that his uncle Max, the brashest and richest of all Melech's sons, has fallen under the spell of his blonde secretary, Miss Holmes, who despises him. These men of the ghetto yearn towards the feminine personifications of what seems a freer world beyond the invisible walls.

But they also turn, like Melech writing his letters to the past, to strange hidden activities that give an illusion of escape into some underground self. Wolf parodies his father's box in the false-bottomed desk where he keeps the coded diaries that record a secret life of terrifying banality, in which he counts his steps, measures his urine, notes his rows with his wife ("average over a twenty-year period— 2.2 quarrels a day") and records it all in elaborate statistics to be hidden away from the world like the objects buried in an Egyptian tomb. From the inhabitants of the ghetto, with their Balzacian obsessions, Noah turns towards the "liberated" assimilationist Jews of his mother's family, the Goldenbergs. At first they seem to him upstanding Canadian mediocrities whom, in his own mental disturbance after his desertion of Miriam, he almost envies.

He finally realized that the secret of their humanity was that each one had a tiny deviation all of his and/or her own. None conformed completely. Marsha, the little bitch, had love being made to her by a McGill quarterback whilst she was trying to hook Noah. (That finally endeared her to him.) His Aunt Rachel obeyed in all things except that she secretly read the most blatantly pornographic literature, and Mrs. Feldman beat her French poodle with a whip. Terror lurked behind their happiness. In fact, they weren't happy at all: they were composed. Truth was adroitly side-stepped, like a dog's excrement on the foot-path.

What Noah now begins to realize is that all he has been fighting against is really so nebulous—and so evil because so nebulous—that his attempt to define himself in opposition can only fail. Each orthodoxy and each conformity survives only because its supporters have found the appropriate evasions that allow them to retain the illusion of individuality, but, while their evasions keep them human, they also make them culpable. The great collective crimes are committed with the consent of men and women who cling to such private caves of withdrawal, who cannot recognize the brutal realities of a world they support by default.

At last Noah understood about the concentration camps. About the Goldenbergs and Harvey. The Germans had told the truth when they said that they hadn't known. They couldn't cope with knowing. Neither could the Goldenbergs. Their crimes varied in dimension, but not in quality.

Noah realizes in the end the need for "some knowledge of himself that was independent of others," for some self-definition that will not merely be in terms of opposition. He must uncover the truth and refuse to live by the tempting evasion. His ruthlessness appears again. By something very near to blackmail he forces his uncle Max to cease exploiting the legend of Wolf Adler the Hero. He accepts as the price of his departure to Europe the probability that his mother will die of heart attack. He appears to have a partial reconciliation with Melech, who had hoped to make him "a Something," but when he leaves, the old man feels his grandson's kiss "like a burn. He touched his cheek and felt that he had been punished."

Noah believes he can turn himself into a real human being by "refusing to take part" in the conspiracy of evasion; he becomes voluntarily an outsider. For Melech, who dominates the last lines of the book, he is merely "Finished," a candidate for God's just punishment, and we can imagine that few of his associates will have regretted his departure. He has been far too disconcerting a companion.

Son of a Smaller Hero is often amusing, but rarely pleasant, and never comforting; Richler would not have wanted us to find it so. His revelation of the ruthlessness of the man who seeks the truth is as deliberate as his exposure of the brutal world where men accept big lies and live by small evasions. Like most good satirists, he has his moments of compassion, but his most convincing tendernesses are those which emerge with the sharp rigours of candour. Richler's best line is taut, twanging, and a little discordant.

A CONVERSATION WITH MORDECAI RICHLER

This conversation took place in September 1956 in London, England. The interviewer was NATHAN COHEN.

COHEN   You're a Canadian writer now living in London, and you've been abroad for several years. Do you think of yourself as an expatriate?

RICHLER   I don't think of myself as an expatriate. I think words like "generation," "expatriate," and on another level "honour" and "love," have become almost advertising executive words, and these labels when attached to writers are very inhibiting and unfortunate. I don't think that writers think of themselves as expatriates or as speaking for their generation or any generation, if they are at all serious.

COHEN   But isn't there such a thing as a Canadian colony here in London of which you're a part? Isn't that an expatriate colony in effect?

RICHLER   In effect it is—yeah. But I left Canada the first time when I was nineteen. Most of the Canadians I know I met here. And this Canadian colony became a fact long after I got here. The novel I am just finishing is about this kind of people and what happens—they don't come over as expatriates or to be expatriates, they just slip into it.

COHEN   Would you say that London is the place where most writers from the English-speaking countries, including the United States, want to come now? Is this the literary centre now?

RICHLER   No.

COHEN   Why do you say that? You sound so definite.

From *Tamarack Review*, No. 2 (Winter 1957); pp. 6-23. By permission of Nathan Cohen.

RICHLER   Well, personally I think much more interesting things are being done in New York. I feel more affinity with the young writers in New York, with Mailer and Algren and William Styron and Herbert Gold. These people interest me much more. The young writers here, like Kingsley Amis—who is very good—still seem to be writing almost provincial undergraduate jokes in a very special context. So if you know England, and even perhaps if you don't, they are quite funny, but they aren't nearly as ambitious as the novels that Mailer. . . . I am not a European writer and I couldn't become one if I stayed here twenty-five years. All my attitudes are Canadian; I'm a Canadian; there's nothing to be done about it.

COHEN   But if you feel that way, aren't you afraid that the time you have spent in London may affect your writing by removing you from the Canadian scene?

RICHLER   No. If I stayed over here for five or even ten years I couldn't be in serious trouble because I could never know England well enough to write about it from the inside. But I have only been here two or three years, and not all that time in England, and I expect to be going back to Canada after a year or two.

COHEN   After Israel? For that matter, what do you want to go to Israel for?

RICHLER   Well, for very special reasons. I was in the Labour Zionist movement, and when we were all about fifteen or sixteen and the war in Israel broke out—we were all going to go—a lot of us didn't, some did. I'd like to see what has happened to those boys who were brought up around St. Lawrence Boulevard, or hung around the poolrooms with me, and shoplifted with me—

COHEN   Who *what* with you?

RICHLER   —who stole bats at Eaton's and who stole softballs at Eaton's. I'd just like to see how they have adjusted to living on communal farms in Israel.

COHEN   Well, now that we're talking about Montreal, tell me when you first started to write.

RICHLER   When I was about fourteen, I guess. You know—foolish things in a very haphazard way. I used to paint. I took a summer course at the Gallery, and I was expected to become a painter. But all I had was facility. I could have become a third-rate commercial artist. I have done third-rate commercial art.

COHEN   Professionally?

RICHLER   Yeah. But you know, just for little advertising firms while I was in college. But I read a book of short stories, a wonderful book we used to use in high school. I can't remember what it was called, but there were wonderful stories in it. There was a story called "The Face on the Wall"—the kind of story that begins with two Englishmen talking in their club, and one of them tells the story of how he was frightened by a face on the wall, and the day the face disappeared the man died. I used to write very romantic stories of this kind.

COHEN   Did you get books at home? Is there any literary background in your family?

RICHLER   Yes, there is. My uncle is a Yiddish writer who is very well known in New York. He used to be a journalist in Toronto and Montreal. He wrote plays and operettas, and he wrote songs. Then he went down to New York, and for a long time he had a sort of Yiddish vaudeville theatre there. He played in his own productions, and so did my aunt. And my grandfather, his father, was a writer. He was a Hassid and a scholar, and he translated—I understand he did the first modern Hebrew translation of the Zohar. It took him about twenty-five years. And he used to write religious texts, and speeches for rabbis.

COHEN   How much formal education did you have? Did you go to university?

RICHLER   I went to Sir George Williams College for two years. I was in an arts course, and I was an English major student. I did very badly in high school, but I was expected to go to Sir George Williams. I was very quickly disappointed. You see, when I went in the veterans were still there, and the people who became my friends were the veterans. There were some very good, very entertaining people among them. But they were leaving the next year, and suddenly I found that all the people I knew and liked had graduated. So I quit.

COHEN   And went to Paris?

RICHLER   Yes, I came to Europe. I cashed in an insurance policy that my mother had been paying for for years—fifty cents a week. I remember now that one of the things I was afraid of at this time was that I did know some writers. These were the people who wrote for and edited *Northern Review*, and I thought it was very important and very good. But a great many of these people, after they got their B.A.'s, seemed to go on to get an M.A. because the B.A. was worth nothing, and then they got their Ph.D.s, and then they taught. Maybe later they would write their novels. And I became quite frightened that if I got a B.A., I'd get an M.A. and then I might try for a Ph.D., and that would be the end. So I decided the best thing was to cut myself off and find out if I could write.

COHEN   You weren't bothered at all when you landed in Paris? I take it you don't speak French?

RICHLER   Very badly.

COHEN   All right. You land in Paris, a huge, sprawling city, very colourful and all the rest of it, but still an absolutely foreign city, and you completely on your own. You didn't have much money—

RICHLER   I had money. I didn't know anyone, and the first three weeks were really miserable, because, you know, Paris is a terribly friendless—Life takes place in the streets, people at the other tables talking and obviously having a good time, and I knew nobody and I was very depressed and lonely and scared. Like most kids I had read a lot about Paris, I had read Hemingway, and it was a terrible disappointment to me at the very beginning. I had reached Saint-Germain-des-Prés, and there was a girl at the corner café reading one of those continental editions of Faulkner's *Sanctuary*, and I thought everyone was very friendly here, and I said "I have just arrived and am looking for a room." And she wouldn't talk to me.

COHEN   You know why, don't you?

RICHLER   She thought I was trying to pick her up. But this was my first experience of Paris. Anyway, about six weeks later I ran into a man—There were about three "little magazines" functioning in Paris then, and one of them was called *Points*. It wasn't very good really, but I ran into the man who was editing it, and he asked me if I had any stories, and I had three very short mood pieces I had written. I gave them to him and got the shock of my life when he printed them.

COHEN   All three?

RICHLER   Yeah. Well, the three of them amounted to about three thousand words. And this was the first time I was published. I wrote a lot of stories, none of which were printed anywhere—

COHEN   What kind of rejections did you get? Just formal blue slips?

RICHLER   No, I got letters. I got letters, and I got printed slips. I got a letter from *The Atlantic Monthly*—I was submitting things to the *Atlantic* and *Harper's* and *Esquire*—I got little letters, friendly letters, which meant a lot. And then I went to Spain, and there in six weeks I wrote a novel. I didn't know much about writing a novel and I never submitted it anywhere. I rewrote it and threw it away. *The Acrobats* began as a short story and ended up as a novel. I don't think I would have submitted that because by this time I was very frightened. But I met Michael Sayers in Paris—

COHEN   He's a playwright, isn't he?

RICHLER   Yes. He read it and recommended that I send it to an agent. Actually it's a very funny story. I came to London and I called the agent, and she gave me an appointment, and I was very disreputable at the time. I needed a haircut and a shave, and I shoved the novel into a long-playing record album and brought it to her.

COHEN   Who is your agent?

RICHLER   Joyce Weiner. And she was very dubious about the whole thing. I was leaving for Canada in two days, and she said that she wouldn't be able to read it for a long time, and that I was very young, and in fact said that she was sure it was no bloody good. And she did start to read it that night and called me at eight o'clock the next morning and asked me to come right down. She talked to me about it for a long time very intelligently and asked me to rewrite it, and she said that she was submitting it the same day to Daniel George who is an editor at Jonathan Cape, not as a submission but to ask his opinion as a friend. He read it, but I left England, and when I arrived in Canada I had a letter from Daniel George saying that he wanted to see it when I rewrote it. I worked for a diaper salesman, and I worked for almost everybody, and finally I got a job in the CBC newsroom in Montreal and re-wrote it. Before Daniel George could see it again, André Deutsch bought it. Walter Allen read it and again I was asked to work on it, and later it was sold to the States.

COHEN   A moment ago you mentioned *Northern Review*, and we've been talking about *The Acrobats*, and this ties in with one of the questions I want to ask you. There are one or two comments in that book which suggest that you don't have a very high opinion of literary and artistic developments in Canada. Has any Canadian writer impressed or influenced you?

RICHLER I think there are some really good writers in Canada, but I think that one of the most significant things about Canadian writing is that what to my mind are the two best novels that have been written in Canada are by Canadians in quotes—*Under the Volcano* by Malcolm Lowry (and he is an Englishman) and *Judith Hearne* by Brian Moore (and he is Irish). But I think Ethel Wilson is a good writer, and I like very much Robertson Davies' *Leaven of Malice*. I think Morley Callaghan was probably the best—I mean when I read his short stories when I was quite young, I was really very impressed, and I think the best stories or prose I have read by an English-Canadian writer who is truly Canadian are those stories of Morley Callaghan's.

COHEN Well, is it true that you don't have a very high opinion of literary and artistic developments in Canada?

RICHLER I haven't got a high opinion of them.

COHEN Why?

RICHLER Because of the special dangers in Canada. The general opinion seems to be that Canadians aren't interested in the arts, but I'm not sure that the lack of interest in Canada is much different than in other countries. And there's a danger in Canada of going quite the other way. I mean this man Lionel Shapiro wrote an article in *Maclean's* that I happened to see a year or so ago, saying that Canada doesn't pay enough attention to Canadian writers in general and Lionel Shapiro in particular. Now I think that if Lionel Shapiro had been American or English, he would be taken for granted—I mean he wouldn't be considered on the literary level as all—just another guy turning out bestsellers very much like sausages. The very fact that he would be asked to write an article about Canadian writing and the lack of attention he has had illustrates the dangers I see in Canada. I mean that Lionel Shapiro is not a serious writer.

COHEN What do you mean by "serious writer"? This is a term I keep running into over here.

RICHLER I'll tell you what I mean. You know there are various motives for writing. Some people write to earn a living and I have nothing against that. But ninety per cent of the books that are published aren't serious, in that they're written as amusements or for the author's financial profit. These people, let's say, are entertainers. Now I think the serious writer is entertaining, but the difference I'd say is that the serious writer is *also* entertaining. He is not an entertainer, he is not writing for money, he is writing from compulsion, I guess.

COHEN Do you consider yourself a serious writer?

RICHLER Yes.

COHEN Are *The Acrobats* and *Son of a Smaller Hero* and the novel you're now writing about Canadians abroad— are these written under compulsion?

RICHLER Yes, they are.

COHEN A compulsion to say what?

RICHLER What but to say what the novels say? I mean to say what I feel about values and about people living in a time when to my mind there is no agreement on values.

COHEN I want to ask you more about this later. But for the time being let's talk a little more about your opinion of the literary life in Canada.

RICHLER Well, just this morning I saw a review in the *New York Times* of Adele Wiseman's novel, and the reviewer mentioned what he thought were the three best first novels of the year, and two of them were by Canadians. One was Adele Wiseman's and the other was Brian Moore's. Sure, there are good writers in Canada. But my point is that there are people of good faith, a very, very limited number, who are interested in Canadian writing, and if the young writer stays in Canada the tremendous danger is that they will help him to over-value himself. In England Adele Wiseman and Brian Moore (if he were here) and myself are three among other promising writers. In Canada there is tremendous excitement now, and I think there is the danger of young writers being overwhelmed by the CBC and by the Establishment and by the universities—

COHEN   By the Establishment? Is there an Establishment in Canada?

RICHLER   I mean being invited to speak, being commissioned to write things. . . . It's dangerous because it's out of proportion. You certainly keep a sense of proportion here and a sense of your own worth among many serious young writers trying to do something.

COHEN   It's obvious that when you wrote *The Acrobats* you never even thought of submitting it to a Canadian publisher, you went to see Joyce Weiner. But did it occur to you then, or has it occurred to you since to submit your novels for first publication to a Canadian publisher?

RICHLER   No. I have had one experience with a Canadian publisher. When *The Acrobats* had been accepted here I was in Canada, and André Deutsch wrote to me to visit the Canadian distributor. I spent a day in Toronto and went to visit him. And the first question this man who distributes books for—well, a dozen very reputable publishers—the first question he asked me about my novel was "Is it a thick book?" Because Canadians like thick books. The second question he asked was are there any Communists in it and is it anti-Canadian? The whole thing was ridiculous. The system of publishing in Canada and the system of awards is just a joke. I think this puts in a capsule everything you might say about the Canadian literary scene officially that last year what is supposed to be the big literary award for a novel went to Lionel Shapiro's *The Sixth of June*.

COHEN   Isn't it a fact that there might be advantages in having your novels published first in Canada, and then submit them over here and in the States?

RICHLER   As a matter of fact, it would be much more profitable. I would get royalties in dollars, and now I get a royalty of the English price, which comes to very little. I make about a nickel on every copy sold in Canada, while if the novels were published in Canada by a Canadian publisher I might get forty cents. But I don't know of any capable editors in Canada, and I don't know any publisher who dares to publish a book in Canada without first sending it out to an American or British firm.

COHEN   Have any of them approached you for first publication of the two novels that were published?

RICHLER   No.

COHEN   Have any of them shown any interest in you?

RICHLER   No.

COHEN   Has anyone in Canada in a position to give you employment shown any interest in you as a writer?

RICHLER   The only organization or people that have been of any help to me at all is the CBC.

COHEN   You mean to say that you have had no requests from magazines or newspapers—

RICHLER   Well, I had a very unfortunate experience. I sent a short story to *Maclean's* which was turned down, but they asked me to submit my second novel, *Son of a Smaller Hero*, for their novel award. I wrote them saying that having read *Maclean's*, I realized they could never publish this kind of book and I thought it was a waste of time for both of us for me to submit it. But they wrote again asking me to submit it, and I sent them a copy of the novel and never thought of it again. Then a letter arrived asking if I could wait a few days and then they would send me a definite decision, and the gist of the letter seemed to be that I had all but won the award. I just couldn't see how they would publish it, and of course in the end they didn't. I don't think they can publish serious novels and I don't think they should pretend they can.

COHEN   You are a Jew of course, and the identification is plain enough in your novels. How does the Jewish cultural and religious tradition affect your writing? You mentioned before your uncle and grandfather.

RICHLER   I'm sure it has a hell of a lot of effect. The problem of writing about Jews is very, very difficult. There is a condescending tradition that the Jew—

COHEN   Where?

RICHLER   Where? In fiction. When the Jew appears, he is sympathetic, down-trodden, he speaks in parables, and he has had a hard time. Or on another level he is a "colourful" character. And I think this is condescending, I think it is a form of anti-Semitism. But when you write about a Jewish businessman whose practices may be as devious and corrupt as his Gentile equivalents, you run into the danger that an anti-Semite may pick up your novel and say: This is true; this is the way the Jews are. This is one of the dangers you run into. One of the things I was most concerned with in *Son of a Smaller Hero* was that it seems to me that class loyalties in Montreal were much stronger than so-called Jewish loyalties or traditions; that the middle-class Jew has much more in common with the middle-class Gentile than he has with the Jew who works for him in his factory. And some people obviously read my novel and thought it was anti-Semitic.

COHEN   Was there a violent reaction from the Jewish community in Canada?

RICHLER   Yes, there was a violent reaction and I expected that and I expected people to be hurt; but what I didn't expect was abuse. My book largely wasn't reviewed in Canada, it was abused. I had written a serious book. In

England it was well received. I don't mind people not liking the book, and some Jewish journals here attacked it. The *Jewish Observer* didn't agree with my arguments and thought it was unfortunate; but they treated it seriously, said that it was very well written. The Montreal *Star* said it should have been published as a paperback and sold under the counter. Now in the Yiddish papers it was also abused, but I don't mind this nearly so much because I think it sprang from deep feeling. These people were genuinely hurt.

COHEN   One of the things that interest me is the copious references to the Talmud, the Torah, to religious precepts and Jewish ritual, and to matters of this kind in both novels. Obviously religion has had a strong influence on you. When you speak of yourself as a Jew, do you include a religious identification?

RICHLER   No. Well, I'm not religious, but my background was an Orthodox one. This is the first generation in our family with no rabbis. I should have been a rabbi.

COHEN   You went of course to cheder, Jewish School?

RICHLER   Yes, I went to parochial school, and at night I went to cheder. I studied Talmud and I studied Modern Hebrew.

COHEN   How many years were you there?

RICHLER   Well, I broke with all this at about thirteen.

COHEN   You broke with it? You mean you just stopped going?

RICHLER   I just stopped going. I stopped wearing a hat. I stopped obeying all the rules and I began to eat food that wasn't Kosher.

COHEN   What about the Jewish writers among your contemporaries? Are you especially interested in them because they're Jewish and write on Jewish themes?

RICHLER   No. But I have a very definite interest in people writing about a background I know well. In other words, if someone else wrote, as someone else surely will, about being brought up in a working-class district in Montreal, I'd be very interested because the experience would be familiar to me. And I was very interested to read other books and see that the pattern is more or less the same in other cities. But outside that, no. Most Jewish writers annoy me because they write about the Jews in a honeyed way. It's like writing about the poor for the rich as Saroyan did to a large extent in his later stories.

COHEN   You said earlier that you felt a much closer sense of kinship with American writers than with English or European writers. Why do you feel this way?

RICHLER   Because I consider myself an American, and the first modern novels I read were American. I read Dos Passos and Hemingway and Fitzgerald and Faulkner, and these are people who influenced me a great deal. And of course my attitudes are American, and even coming here is a North American convention, and I am not really much influenced by the young English novelists. And when I said that American novelists are more ambitious, what I mean is they work on a much broader canvas and with much more freedom because the society is much more flexible. They circulate on different social levels, and they can write about them.

COHEN   As far as your actual techniques are concerned, are you trying to model yourself on any writer in particular?

RICHLER   No, of course not.

COHEN   Why do you say of course not?

RICHLER   Because the criterion for any writer in the end is: Could this book have been written by someone else? Writers like Faulkner and Hemingway and Céline have understood this; and they have almost created their own vocabulary, their own approach to language, so that when you look at a page by Faulkner or Hemingway or

Céline—and of course there are many others—not that many—you know it is their book, whether it is good or bad. You look at a page, and you know that no one else could have written it. It is their window, and this is the state for a writer to reach.

COHEN   Let's forget your novels for the time being and get back to you as an individual. How have you managed to make a living since you became a writer?

RICHLER   I've been a professional for, let's say, four years.

COHEN   You are what now? Twenty-three?

RICHLER   Twenty-five. For four years—I've been earning a living for the past two years. Until that time my wife worked, and I wasn't earning a living.

COHEN   You didn't make any money from your first novel?

RICHLER   As a matter of fact, I made a surprising amount on my first novel because it was widely translated and published as a pocket book. I made about $2,000. And here I was able to live on it. We managed. I have only been earning a living in the last two years and not out of my novels but by doing occasional television work or films or journalism. I haven't yet been able to make a living strictly from my novels.

COHEN   What have been the sales of your novels?

RICHLER   Well, *The Acrobats* sold 2,000 copies in its English edition, and that includes Canada, where it sold about 200 copies. *Son of a Smaller Hero* went into a second printing, and it has sold about 3,500 copies. In Canada it has sold about 800 so far.

COHEN   Has it been turned into a pocket book too?

RICHLER   No. It hasn't yet been published in the States.

COHEN   How does one get one's novel published as a pocket book? What was it, for example, that sold *The Acrobats* to a pocket book publisher?

RICHLER   Well, it probably sold for the wrong reasons. It sold because there was a big scene in a brothel. I think so anyway.

COHEN   What did you get paid for the pocket book edition?

RICHLER   The advance wasn't very good, but it was $1,500, half of which goes to the publisher of the original edition. I'm afraid that American publishers have the habit now when they take a book of thinking right away whether it will be a pocket book because this underwrites the original edition to some extent.

COHEN   Do you get any advance money from a publisher when you're writing a novel?

RICHLER   I can. But as I say, I've been earning a living these past two years, so I haven't.

COHEN   You say that the way you make a living is through journalism and writing for TV and the films, and things like that. What effect does this have on you as a novelist —on your profession?

RICHLER   It consumes time. You see, as far as I'm concerned, because it's difficult to earn your living as a novelist, the first thing to find out is the easiest and most painless way of earning a living. It seems to me much more painless to write a hack TV script and earn enough money to live six months than to work in a factory or take a summer job.

COHEN   Don't you think this sort of writing is likely to have an unfortunate effect on your writing and your thinking?

RICHLER   Not unless you overdo it. I've only done this work when I needed the money, and then I've looked around for the quickest and easiest job I could get.

COHEN   How do you get these jobs? Do you dream things up and go out and sell them, or do people come to you?

RICHLER   It varies. I was once offered a steady job which would pay me in one week what the advance was on my first novel—£100 a week, writing for TV, a steady job —and I turned it down. This is exactly what I don't want.

COHEN   Don't you want to earn a lot of money?

RICHLER   No. I want money to write with. I will do almost anything to have money to write with—to write what I want. TV fills a function as a sort of Guggenheim Foundation for me. I've been lucky enough to find quick jobs when I needed the money. I've written for comedians, I've done all sorts of little things.

COHEN   I know that you have also written some TV plays and are working on a film. Do you find that you consciously write below your peak when you're working for these other media?

RICHLER   Most of the TV work I've done I've written for the boss, the same way you write letters for the boss. I did one TV play here, I didn't use my own name, and I thought I knew exactly what they wanted. I did it and I got paid for it, and that was that. Now journalism is different. I am writing a monthly newsletter from London for the *Montrealer*. It's different work than writing fiction and I enjoy it, so this is something else.

COHEN   You said something earlier about left-wing and right-wing attitudes, and I want to go into that now. You're interested in politics?

RICHLER   Yeah.

COHEN   Are you a left-winger, as it were?

RICHLER   I guess so. Yes. I'm a socialist.

COHEN   When did you become a socialist?

RICHLER   In college.

COHEN   Do you consider that you have much in common let's say with the socialist novelists of the Thirties who idealized and glorified the poor man, the common man?

RICHLER   I don't think so, but a lot of critics thought that of my first novel. I happened to fall in with a group of people much older than I am, in a series of groups that were very active in the Thirties. People who are about forty right now. They had bet their lives on politics, and something happened to them, the politics is no longer there. At the age of forty or thereabouts it has altered, and yet it was all they had. I am very concerned with this kind of experience and it's what I am writing about right now.

COHEN   What is the name of your new novel?

RICHLER   *A Choice of Enemies.*

COHEN   You referred before to the fact that you're fascinated in writing about the breakdown of values. Does this mean that you yourself have no values, or is there a set of values you feel should emerge or is emerging from this breakdown?

RICHLER   I think what is emerging from this breakdown is a much more complicated and closely held personal standard of values. Even in small things. I think we are coming back to a very personal and basic set of values because the exterior values have failed. There has been a collapse of absolute values, whether that value was God or Marx or gold. We are living at a time when superficially life seems meaningless, and we have to make value judgements all the time, it seems in relation to nothing. Do you understand what I am saying? This seems to me the big problem.

COHEN   What are you trying to say about it? That it is true? Or simply to reflect it? Or what?

RICHLER   What I am looking for are the values with which in this time a man can live with honour.

COHEN   Well, you said a while ago that you were prepared to live with honour as far as your writing was concerned, but that you were prepared to do almost anything you could to continue writing. Isn't that a contradiction?

RICHLER No. It's not a contradiction. It's a personal adjustment. I mean that if you need work, or if you are working for someone—or even in very restricted terms you need three meals a day—you can't go around telling people what you think of them all the time.

COHEN You do a fair amount of that.

RICHLER I will do a lot in small to be able to write my novels. I have gone into TV offices and taken part in ridiculous conferences and I have nodded and smiled when expected to. I've done these things. It's just something I have to do.

COHEN How do you think one can live with honour in a society where all the values have broken down?

RICHLER I'm not sure.

COHEN So your books to an extent are a reflection of this search for honour? Let's talk specifically. What is André searching for in *The Acrobats* that can be described as honour?

RICHLER Well, at that stage André is probably really suffering a very sensitive reaction to all the corruption about him and hasn't as a character reached the positive stage of the search when he dies. He is still at a period when everything disgusts him.

COHEN While we're on *The Acrobats*, an unfriendly critic might say that book is very noticeably a young man's novel, in the sense that it reflects so many contemporary literary and social attitudes. Or to put it another way, it has a young man's despair of the world, and yet the last word in the novel—a word which seems a little rhetorical in the context—is "hope." After three or four years, what do you yourself think of *The Acrobats*?

RICHLER Well, I actually reread it recently because I did a TV play of it. I would no longer have written that book of course. But you know, I'm on the defensive; it's mine.

COHEN   Is it a good book?

RICHLER   I'll take the rap. No, I don't think it's a good book.

COHEN   What do you think is wrong with it?

RICHLER   I think it's too wild, the attitudes aren't real, they are undigested. I still feel the same as I did about the last part though. I don't think it's rhetorical. I think this is essentially a time of hope. But no—I don't think it's a very good novel.

COHEN   This method you've chosen for yourself as a full-time professional writer—it's pretty risky and dangerous, in an economic sense, and I suppose you might say in a psychological sense as well. Wouldn't it be better to take a job and write in your free time? What is the advantage of the method you've chosen?

RICHLER   Well, I have a certain pride in being a professional. As I said before, I've done hack work. I don't like it, I don't enjoy it, but I can do these jobs if necessary. I think too many writers have taken refuge in the Academy. They are lecturing on creative writing, or they have taken jobs and are cut off.

COHEN   But don't you find that you're moving, in certain circles that cut you off from life in the large?

RICHLER   I have been for a year because I wanted to. I got very interested in these people and in this whole left-wing quarrel, which after I thought about it for a while seemed to me less of an argument of principle and more of an argument of power, even in the States.

COHEN   Will you explain that?

RICHLER   Well, the people who have been blacklisted and who have left the States protested that this was a violation of freedom of speech and democracy, and I signed petitions and I believed this. And now it seems to me that it was an argument of power, it was a question of *their* freedom of speech and *their* democratic rights being threatened. And that in reality they are just as intolerant as the people who are in power, without the authority, which makes them a little worse, a little less magnanimous—You see, my new novel, very baldly, is about a refugee from East Berlin who falls in with the people who have been blacklisted in America and are living in London, and they treat him eventually in the same way as they were treated, and they treat him that way because of his political beliefs. I believe that the essence of this whole thing was one of power.

COHEN   We haven't talked about your methods of writing at all. How do you write a novel? Do you plan it in advance or what?

RICHLER   I plan it to some extent—But I probably write a novel in the most wasteful way. This novel I have just about finished will be about 100,000 words when it is finally done. I intend to cut another five or ten thousand. Now I've written at least 200,000 words over two years for this novel, I have rewritten scenes and chapters six or seven or eight times that I have already thrown out. So I go about writing a novel in a very wasteful fashion. I start with the people—

COHEN   Do you draw up a list of characters or something along this line?

RICHLER   I know the people and the problems I want to write about, and I make up a story of some kind, which I very rarely stick to, and then I develop the story. Actually for the first time in this novel I'm really trying to tell a story.

COHEN   How many hours a day do you work? When do you start?

RICHLER   I work about five hours a day. I work all morning from nine to twelve and then I work for a couple of hours in the afternoon.

COHEN   You rewrite as you're working?

RICHLER   Yes, I work in a very uneven and haphazard way. With this novel I got to page 150 about four times, and then started all over again. It started as a story beginning in Munich and taking place in Paris. Now there is still a chapter in Munich, but most of the novel takes place in London, and there is a brief scene in Paris. Characters have disappeared. There were far too many of them.

COHEN   From what you've said I gather that you are extremely self-critical and that you go over your work as analytically as you can. Do you submit it to other people while it's in progress for their opinions?

RICHLER   No. But soon it will go to my publisher. The three partners will read it, maybe Walter Allen will read it, and Francis Wyndham, their literary adviser now, will read it. If sensible and reasonable suggestions are made—if certain things aren't clear—I am willing to cut or make reasonable changes. I will not substitute an ending or make something happy that is sad. I am poor on construction, and I am willing to take criticism and suggestions. My publisher, André Deutsch, is very reputable. They publish fewer books than most, there are very few independent publishers left here, but when a critic gets one of their books he will look at it anyway. They have developed a very good reputation for bringing on young writers.

COHEN   Do you like talking about your novels while you're writing them?

RICHLER   No. Absolutely not!

HEROES OF THE RICHLER VIEW

NATHAN COHEN

Four years have passed since Mordecai Richler's first novel was published. His subsequent output includes two more novels, a number of short stories, two hour-long television plays and twice as many half-hour films, and reviews and articles in magazines as assorted and opposite as the Bevanite weekly *Tribune* and *The Montrealer*. Undiscovered as yet in the United States (though his first novel was reprinted as a pocketbook), he can lay claim to mention in the fiction surveys of the English quality press and journals. To the serious young writer in England, such recognition, however tentative and non-committal, means that he may hope to gain admission into the official world of letters.

Here in Canada few reviewed and only a few hundred bought *The Acrobats*. Sales quadrupled for *Son of a Smaller Hero*, with its candidly unflattering mural of Jewish middle-class life in Montreal. The new novel, *A Choice of Enemies*, is selling fairly well and has earned considerable critical notice. *The Toronto Star* and *The Montreal Daily Star* were favourably disposed, on balance, to his story of leftwing American and Canadian expatriates in London. It was summarily dismissed, however, in the Toronto *Globe and Mail's* influential Saturday book page, and obtained lukewarm approval from the CBC program "Critically Speaking."

Writing novels dealing searchingly with indigenous Canadian motifs, or addressed primarily to Canadian readers, imposes more than the normal share of hardships

From *Tamarack Review*, No. 6 (1957); pp. 47-60. By permission of the author.

on any writer hoping to make a living from his craft here. There is to begin with the limited market at home, and the infinitesimal interest abroad. More important, of course, is the absence in English-speaking Canada of any positive literary tradition and heritage, the want of a vigorous, discriminating body of cultural thought and opinion. In an interview published in the Winter 1957 edition of this magazine, Mordecai Richler discussed the difficulties as they affect him, frankly and at some length.

One reason for his decision to live in England and be published there, he explained was that "if the young writer stays in Canada, the tremendous danger is that [people of good faith, interested in Canadian writing] will help him to overvalue himself." The danger exists, too, of the young writer's (Richler is twenty-six) being overwhelmed by invitations from the CBC and the Establishment (which he did not define but by which presumably he means the intelligentsia or the academic, publishing, and mass-media communities) to speak and write things. "It's dangerous because it's out of proportion. You certainly keep a sense of proportion [in England] and a sense of your own worth among serious young writers trying to do things." Another reason for seeking English publication is that more prestige and opportunity accrues to the writer. Publication in Canada first or alone offers no special advantage.

At present Richler still depends on television, film, and magazine assignments—which he himself describes as hack journalism—to maintain himself. The only justification, he said in his interview, is that he can earn enough in six months to be free to spend the remaining half-year on his next novel. Since such work demands a flattening out and a blurring of standards, is there not a likelihood that it will stultify his perceptions and creative resolve? He did not think so. Nor did he see any compromise in integrity between writing what he hopes is honest, worthwhile fiction with one hand and what he knows is boilerplate with the other. "It's not a contradiction. It's a personal adjustment."

When Richler gave the interview, his ideas about the menace of Canadian exposure were largely theoretical. He had been away from home for several years; his business contacts were few. Recently, however, he returned for a two-month visit. He was warmly welcomed by the CBC and the Establishment and was invited to speak and write things. Many of these requests he accommodated. Just how tarrying with the lotus-eaters and acknowledging their siren call will affect him as a writer will now, one assumes, be put to a direct test.

There is no doubt in Mordecai Richler's mind that he is a serious writer. The other kind, he pointed out in the interview, writes his stories for personal profit and the reader's momentary diversion. The serious writer entertains too, but "the difference is that he is *also* entertaining." Primarily he writes to illuminate, to get rid of a compulsion or at least to voice it. Mordecai Richler's compulsion is to say what he feels about values and "about people living in a time when . . . there is no agreement on values." Specifically "there has been a collapse of absolute values, whether that value was Marx or God or gold. We are living in a time when superficially life seems meaningless, and we have to make value judgements all the time, it seems in relation to nothing."

To explain this predicament is part of his novels' intention. Their other purpose, he said, is to find those values with which today a man can live honourably. Are there any such values? After first saying he was not sure, he later declared, "I think what is emerging . . . is a much more complicated and closely held personal standard of values. . . . We are coming back to a very personal and basic set of values." There was no further elucidation.

So, bleakly and uncertainly, speaks Mordecai Richler. Unquestionably he is the master's voice of his three heroes, articulating their drives and his books' underlying thesis.

Each novel depicts as hero someone caged in a hopelessly corrupt society; to stay on is to go mentally sterile and die, to quit it demands singular comprehension and a martyr's courage. Driven by his demon, André Bennett of *The Acrobats* leaves the arid Canadian soil for the bloodsoaked Spanish earth. Spain is where the killing began, he remarks, and perhaps here he will find the answers to his questions. Similarly the eponymous nonconformist of *Son of a Smaller Hero* wrests himself free of the tribal clutch and embarks for England in search of a meaningful existence.

The basic pattern of *A Choice of Enemies* is the same, with one mild variation. From the beginning André Bennett and Noah Adler know that theirs is a decadent, dying world. When we meet Norman Price he is certain that he has a virtuous, satisfactory code. A left-wing liberal, midway between party member and fellow traveller in attitude, Norman Price is the Canadian-born son of a surgeon who died in the services of the Spanish Loyalists. Norman lived and taught in the United States until a Senate summons made him a Fifth Amendment celebrity. Now he lives in London, where he secretly doctors film scenarios and writes pocketbook thrillers for American consumption under a pseudonym. His discovery that his fellow refugees from McCarthyism are every inch as unprincipled and intolerant as their persecutors destroys his sense of security and precipitates his quest for a new Holy Grail.

These are unfamiliar elements and people for a Canadian novel. We have several skilled writers living among us (Ethel Wilson, Robertson Davies, Morley Callaghan, and Brian Moore come to mind at once) and a handful of novelists dutifully trying to mine native sources for inspiration (Hugh MacLennan is the prime example). Mordecai Richler is alone, however, in asserting that he deals with the larger issues of our age, and from the vantage-point of one raised and spiritually tutored in

Canada. Since in addition he seems to be mirroring those emotions so manifest in the literature of other English-language countries—symbolized by England's Angry Young Men and the beat generation of the United States—then a hopeful interest in him is bound to exist among people of good faith concerned with Canadian writing. No-one will deny that we need writers prepared to look unsparingly around them, and within themselves, to volunteer judgements and to draw conclusions.

But is Mordecai Richler really in touch with his time?

Here one runs head-on into a curious discrepancy between what Mordecai Richler says he is writing about, what his heroes think they are railing against, and his novels' actual content. Granted that he employs the idiom and a few of the ideas ventilated by his American and English contemporaries, in terms of social viewpoint, feeling, and literary style Mordecai Richler unmistakably harks back to an earlier period. The best evidence for this is his preoccupation with the Marxist mirage and the Jewish middle-class family unit, the latter as it evolved in the East European *shtetl* and later in North America.

Neither is an issue of current validity. The subject of friction between first- and second-generation Jews and their American-born children is a noticeably exhausted one with such prominent American Jewish writers as Saul Bellow, Harvey Swados, Herbert Gold, Arthur Miller, Bernard Malamud, and Norman Mailer. Theirs is no cowardly neglect, no parvenu passion to disclaim their skullcap and prayer-shawl antecedents. In point of fact, this particular narrative vein began to peter out after the First World War with the cessation of the mass migrations from Russia and Poland. It dried up altogether by the time of the second world bloodbath.

Apt though it was then for the Ab Cahans and Mike Golds and Meyer Levins, appropriate as it may be for nostalgists like Charles Angoff, the problem of first- and second-Jewish-generation relationships is today an

archaism. The Jewish family unit has been totally recon-
stituted; the Yiddish-language daily press is a spent,
shrinking force; the tragic propensity of Jewish intellectuals to idealize the Soviet Union because anti-Semitism
was legally forbidden has evaporated in the wake of the
Soviet campaign against cosmopolitanism and the pogrom
disclosures; the synagogue is now not a religious, but a
social centre, and fifty-seven different brands of Zionism
vie among the faithful. Not that there is any scarcity of
conflicts confronting the Jew as an individual or as a
member of a group that would make the legitimate stuff
of fiction. The point is that Mordecai Richler's concept
excludes the middle-class Jew (the *lower* upper-middle-
class Jew, to be precise) as he really is. *Son of a Smaller
Hero* negotiates an obsolescent theme; moreover, the
process is carried on in dated fashion.

Everything about the novel has an aura of ancient
history. Consider, for example, the patriarch Melech
Adler. He clings fiercely to old-country precepts, convinced
that the *goyim* he lives among and does business with are
biding their opportunity to pounce and rob and cheat,
and perhaps kill. Once he dreamed of being a scribe, of
writing by hand on parchment the sacred words of the
Old Testament; how his heart swelled with pride when
one of his sons married a Rabbi's daughter.

Now he walks alone, under a darkening nimbus of dis-
may. His children are indifferent to their faith. Resentful
of his authority, they simulate filial respect and eagerly
assume as their own *goyische* customs and attitudes; one
indeed is a whoremonger and arsonist. Furthest removed
from the old man is his grandson Noah. Melech had especially high hopes for him. But Noah too plows a lonely
furrow and accepts Melech's shrill enmity and estrangement as part of the price to be paid for freedom.

In the context of the North American world we live in,
there is infinitely more truth, more reality, in a *Marjorie*

Morningstar or *Remember Me to God*. For all their expediency, at least Herman Wouk and Myron Kaufman chronicle the mores and conventions of a live and identifiable social stratum.

His attachment to Marxism is also part of Mordecai Richler's backward look.

To be sure there is a voluminous and continuing literature of disillusionment with Marxism, some of it fiction. The postwar period has produced its due quota of such books, and now that Howard Fast has issued his *mea culpa* we may expect a story from him dramatizing his bitter odyssey. What counts is that writers like Koestler and Orwell and Silone and Wright and Fast speak from experience. They espoused the Communist movement because their countries were convulsed by revolution, or because the depression convinced them of the need for a planned totalitarian economy, or because it seemed to them to be the only workable alternative to the threat of Fascism. Members of a generation that came of age between two world wars, their involvement and anger over Communism spring from the fact of participation.

In a sense that explains why they and the current generation of English and American writers have such trouble in communicating. To the latter, Marxism has never had any special fascination. For them to judge people and events by a Marx-Engels-Lenin yardstick, or to see in the deflation of the Stalin idolatry and the breakdown of the Marxist ideal a telling commentary on conditions today, is a notion too preposterous to consider further. To Augie March and Jimmy Porter, the Communist man is as remote as the cigar-store Indian and as meaningless. Not that they are unaware of it, and one often finds mention of a Communist flirtation in serious modern fiction. The event serves principally as an incident in the hero's experience, or as exposition to enrich the story texture. The most generous verdict the diehard

Communist or the disillusioned ex-Communist and sympathizer bewailing their lost faith are likely to evoke is a measure of cool pity.

Historically the intellectuals' *entente* with Communism and the various popular fronts reached its zenith during the Spanish Civil War and blew up, save for the odd latecomer like Howard Fast, with the Soviet-German Pact of 1939. In no way is it central to the prevailing social and literary temper.

With Mordecai Richler, on the other hand, it is insistently germane and prior, His judgement of people is determined by a rough Communist rule of thumb; people who have money and property or seek their acquisition belong to the lowest rung of his social edifice. Again, although he was the merest youngster when it happened, through his books there runs a persistent lament that the Spanish Civil War was the last occasion when one could take sides. But were pro-Communist and pro-Fascist sides the only ones to be taken? And where did he get the idea that Communist policy concentrated solely on the expulsion of Franco and his forces from Spain? Let him read George Orwell and catch up with that sad chapter of our century.

In his review of *A Choice of Enemies*, Walter O'Hearn described Mordecai Richler as a political novelist. The designation is only partly correct. The Richler vision embraces left-wing politics only, and the only type of left-wing politics and thinking that his novels appraise with any seriousness has a strong Marxist impulse. At that, it is a Marxism emotionally approached. There are few Communist characters in the books, and they are endowed with a blatantly bookish vocabulary. The impression grows that the author's contact with the ideology and its practitioners is based mostly on hearsay and casual encounters. Fundamentally his point is that the message of the Communist Manifesto formed our last chance to have something to believe in, something that gave the right answers to all questions. Now it has failed, and nothing remains. First went God, then gold, then Marx.

Now certainly Mordecai Richler has every right to concentrate on these matters. Only the writer can decide what material he should deal with. The people he feels are worth studying, the strains he cares to analyse and force and interpret, the dark corners of the human condition he chooses to light up—all are fitting grist for his mill. But he always takes the risk that his findings will be old and far from freshly seen, that they lack the broader, more universal meaning his limited experience suggests to him.

The salient fact about Mordecai Richler's blasting instruments (heavy irony, political attitudinizing, a pious taking for granted of one's superiority and greater wisdom) and his targets for attack is that of themselves they refute his belief that he is coping, squarely and frankly, with the relevant dilemmas of our time.

Conceivably ours is a moribund civilization. Undoubtedly Communism in practice has made a mockery of its professed purpose. To be sure it is immensely difficult for any man wishing to do so now to live with honour and integrity (when was it otherwise?). Still there is nothing in Mordecai Richler's novels to corroborate these agonized claims. The world he inspects in *Son of a Smaller Hero* is defunct, that excoriated in *A Choice of Enemies* never existed. His heroes fling themselves vehemently against enemies that disappear as one approaches them. Small wonder that his heroes have so much trouble enunciating what they are against, and are inarticulate in stating what they are for.

The backward and retrospective view expressed in Mordecai Richler's novels does not make it necessarily inaccurate; a writer does not need a sound knowledge of ideas and social facts to be a sound writer. Whenever Mordecai Richler abjures pontification and devotes himself to a concrete milieu and clearly-conceived experience, he reveals a commendable talent for honest communication.

There are lengthy sections in *Son of a Smaller Hero*—a tawdry funeral ceremony, a family meeting, a furtive visit by some Jewish youngsters to the beach of a restricted Gentile resort, a description of the mopping-up operations after a fire—that are boldly told and true. Certain of the book's *dramatis personae* are closely watched and conveyed, especially the smaller hero, Noah Adler's father. Wolf's degradation, the littleness of his mind, are spelled out meticulously in a secret diary that Noah finds after his father's death. In this journal Wolf Adler reports in childish code his ambitions and daily activities. One part tabulates how much time he spends working, sleeping, eating, defecating, quarrelling with his wife. It takes imagination to get inside so mean a mind.

A Choice of Enemies has moments too when the author displays his story-telling qualities. Jolted by the knowledge that Sally McPherson's lover, Ernest, is also his brother's killer, Norman Price has an amnesia attack that begins with a nightmare hallucination in a railway depot. Price's adventures unfold in a series of brief, spurting, overlapping images created with urgent, frightening momentum.

In that same book Charlie Lawson, a Hollywood grub and peripheral member of the expatriate community, takes off his mask long enough to admit to himself and to Norman Price what he is really like. A self-portrait of the shoddy deterioration of a shoddy man, it is the only instance in all of Richler's writings where a character stirs our sympathy for a wasted life.

Even in *The Acrobats* there are sporadically true glimpses into background and character. They don't relieve the lurid melodrama, the hero's foot-lights melancholy, or the sweeping philosophical generalizations by people stupendously ill-equipped to render them, but they do provide moments of distraction. The bordello sequence adds nothing to the story, true. All the same it is effectively related, as in Barney Larkin's apprehensive excitement at being in the place.

Mordecai Richler is especially adept at conjuring up the squalor of an environment. Dirt and physical ugliness are constantly itemized in his stories, and often used as metaphors and similes. "Night squeezed them like black-heads out of the face of the city." "Truth was adamantly sidestepped, like a dog's excrement on the footpath." He has other mannerisms. There are always filmstyle flash-backs, each of his heroines has small breasts; his business-men are forever itching and sweating; and his characters invariably ask one another about God at cocktail parties.

Unfortunately, his determination to make significant remarks is forever interfering with his craftsmanship and getting in his characters' way. Indeed it is rather presump-tuous to consider the figures populating his books as flesh-and-blood people with their own minds and wills. "A human being is to be approached with a sense of wonder," we are told in *The Acrobats*. Excellent advice, but Morde-cai Richler has no use for it. Most of the men and women who pass through his pages are, by design, empty, trivial, disgusting, happy to vegetate in the safe cage of traditional principles, alarmed beyond belief by the perilous freedom of truth-seeking. They are so small, so worthless, so obvi-ously (according to him) undeserving of compassion, that they are not worth caring about.

That Mordecai Richler is unable to see, and project, people as individuals is most demonstrable in the repeti-tion of characters from novel to novel. Charlie Lawson, of *A Choice of Enemies*, appeared before in *Son of a Smaller Hero* as the culture-conscious professor and cuckold Theo Hall. Larkin, the foul-mouthed and foul-minded tourist visiting Spain with a gentile wife in *The Acrobats* is indis-tinguishable from Noah's uncle, Max, in *Son of a Smaller Hero*, a manufacturer with a gentile mistress. Sonny Winkelmann, the expatriates' leader in *A Choice of*

Enemies, is simply an up-to-date version of the grandfather in *Son of a Smaller Hero*.

Then there are his women. Interestingly Mordecai Richler's novels deal with a man-dominated society; his treatment of the opposite sex suggests at the very least a deep distrust and contempt. Two kinds of female occupy his attention: the woman who takes for granted that an unpleasant time in bed is the contractual consideration for material security (Larkin's wife in *The Acrobats*, Margaret in *Son of a Smaller Hero*), and the woman who believes that happiness is only attainable through sexual gratification. The latter constitutes his heroine. Whether named Toni or Miriam or Sally, she happily defies society's wrath to achieve her purpose.

Miriam in *Son of a Smaller Hero* and Sally in *A Choice of Enemies* follow a conspicuously similar course. After meeting Noah, several years her junior, Miriam leaves her husband to live with him. For a time they are blissful in each other's company. When Noah goes away, Miriam returns to Theo and engages in a perfunctory pursuit of bedroom excitement. For Sally McPherson life begins with the delicious expectation of going to bed with Norman. Then Ernest comes on the scene and she falls madly in love with him. When he runs away she becomes available to a sex-hungry writer. At that Mordecai Richler is kind to her. He condemns Miriam to a withering away. When Sally becomes pregnant, he kills her off.

Essentially Mr. Richler's heroines are temporary pillows for his protagonists to lean on. Weak-minded creatures, they are stepping-stones leading his truth-seekers toward their freedom bridge.

The characteristic hero of the contemporary English novel is a young man educated beyond his station, resolved to find a comfortable niche for himself within an existing, although shrinking, class structure. He regrets, or is indifferent to, the absence of good causes. His American counterpart has made peace with the idea that the American dream and democratic myth have gone the way of the steamboat and the crackerbarrel. He is tough-minded on the surface and soft as butter underneath. He wants terribly to belong, to be accepted, even if only by other people who don't belong. At the same time he is determined not to get caught up in the larger social and economic currents.

Contrast them with Mordecai Richler's nonconformist and angry warrior.

In each of his novels, the Richler hero is an artistically-inclined Canadian with a deep aversion to Canadian culture and a conviction that the society he lives in is a meretricious fraud. Each comes from a comfortably well-to-do home and has an acutely unsatisfied wish for a father-friend, an older man to whom he can turn to for advice and a guide for action when he is perplexed. Each looks to a woman (mother, mistress) for affection, and gets himself involved in a relationship that only means trouble. Each takes it upon himself to interfere in others' lives. Finally, for all his woes, each wins what is at best a nominal emancipation. André Bennett does not even secure that. His wanderings are terminated by death at the hands of an ex-Nazi. Norman Price simply exchanges one bickering, demeaning world for another; his future entails a complete ossification of personality. As for Noah Adler, he is just the André Bennett of the first novel at an earlier stage. Noah is going to Europe to find something to believe in, to look for truths. If a Nazi does not kill him, his uncontrollable penchant for self-analysis surely will.

The Richler heroes have other likenesses. Thus, they never question the values they condemn. They just *know* they are bad. But how and why they fail, and by what means the light dawned on the hero and enabled him to grasp their falsity, we are never actually told.

As an example of the insufficiency of his heroes' value judgements, take the appraisal of the Canadian scene in

Mordecai Richler's books. Canada in them consists of the Jewish ghetto in Montreal and a few adjacent neighbourhoods, a third-rate university and the attached teaching community, and a CBC television studio in Toronto. This minute landscape is enough, nevertheless, to make André Bennett sure that to remain in Canada bodes his spiritual obliteration. Neither he nor Noah Adler ever considers finding out what makes the rest of their city tick, of investigating say the French-language population and culture surrounding them. Each takes for granted that the small subsection of it he has inherited is a microcosm, not just of the city but of the country. Noah is in a panic that he might turn into an upstanding, conservative man "speeding toward Canadian mediocrity, toward an identity which would allow him to pass unrecognized." He would agree too with the observation in *A Choice of Enemies* that, among Canadians, "there was no equivalent of the Canadian dream to boost or knock. The Canadian dream, if there was such a puff, was how do I get out?"

Although Norman Price sometimes thinks of Canada, he never thinks of going back. Charlie Lawson does, a prospect that fills him with dread. "Here's one guy who doesn't want to be a whale in that little pond," he says of himself and the notion of settling down again in Toronto. The Canadians we meet in *A Choice of Enemies* are uncomfortable, isolated, disinherited in exile. But going home seems to them an even more wretched punishment.

It may be they are right, but Mr. Richler makes a poor case on their behalf. The dislike of Canada expressed in his novels does not issue from any genuinely-felt injury or effort to discover what this country is like, what elements hold it together, however shakily, or the nature of its identity such as that is. The unhappy truth is that Mordecai Richler is proffering what is scarcely more than the hit-and-miss, insubstantial chitchat of a pseudo-intellectual tea party as definitive, basic reasoning.

Here is the cruellest irony: the charges the heroes of the Richler view make against their antagonists apply, with equal validity, to themselves. They are selfish, oblivious to human dignity, cold, insensitive, conscienceless, wantonly destructive of personal relations. They have no nobility of spirit. Indeed, they are worse than the people around them since they presume to know better and insist on their superiority. Neither Nemesis nor Galahad, they run an erratic, footless course from anarchy to futility. Mordecai Richler is correct when he declares that few of his people are worth caring about, although there is more to most of them than he realizes. But he is wrong to suppose that his heroes are admirable exceptions. Alas, they are worth caring about the least of all. This is the weakness that causes the scaffolding of each of his novels to totter and give way. With three novels to his credit, it is no longer feasible to think of Mordecai Richler as a beginning writer or to cushion criticism of his work by reason of his youth. It was possible to do so with *The Acrobats* and *Son of a Smaller Hero*, since they were so inherently autobiographical. Under the circumstances the slovenly, undisciplined craftsmanship, the unsettling ambivalence of thought, the contrived violence and abundant bedwetting were understandable, if not pardonable.

A Choice of Enemies suggests that the faults are more deeply ingrained in Mordecai Richler as a writer than was first suspected. In respect to the ratio of felicities and failings, the book is if anything a retrogressive step. There are too few virtues, the weaknesses are the same as before. *There has been no improvement*. Perhaps Mordecai Richler's main trouble is his continued infatuation with the idea of dealing with ideas, with the value of writing stories about values. In a talk he gave two years ago at a rather pointless university conference of Canadian writers, Morley Callaghan said: "There are two kinds of writers: the one who tries to see the world out of his own eyes, and the other one, the commercial writer, who tries to see the world out of the eyes of others." Mordecai Richler, we know, wants to be the first but is showing a regrettable tendency to become the second.

A CHOICE OF CERTAINTIES

PETER DALE SCOTT

Those who like to study the trends and folkways of Canadian letters will not have missed Nathan Cohen's study of Mordecai Richler in the Winter issue of *The Tamarack Review*. This article, we should be thankful, had nothing to do with the too common fabrication of swans from Canada geese. But the problem of the Canadian artist—which was introduced in Richler's latest novel as a kind of comic relief—is taken up by Mr. Cohen with disarming earnestness. By the time he has finished, we are faced in fact with a second problem: the problem of the Canadian reviewer. One is interested, not only in Mr. Cohen's judgements, but in the perspective which they reveal. It is, apparently, "backward" to show any interest in Marxism, while it is downright superficial to show so little interest, indeed such flippancy, about Toronto. "As an example of the insufficiency of his heroes' value-judgements," we are told, "take the appraisal of the Canadian scene in Mordecai Richler's books." None of these heroes "ever considers finding out what makes the rest of their city tick, of investigating say the French-language population and culture surrounding them."

This type of criticism may very well be "distinctively Canadian." I am sure the English Sunday papers found something un-British about *Look Back in Anger*; still, they may have hesitated before suggesting that Jimmy Porter should get off it by investigating, say, the Welsh-language population and what makes them tick. Meanwhile, Mr. Cohen's convictions have made him mistake his facts. André Bennett is *not* sure "that to remain in

From *Tamarack Review*, No. 8 (1958); pp. 73-82. By permission of the author.

Canada bodes his spiritual obliteration." The point of solid interest in *The Acrobats* is precisely the progress from such a state of affairs. The crux of the novel, and André's liberation from uncertainty, comes when he awakens to the half-shaped need to act, the "dignity that was truly wanted": it is at this point he realizes that he must get back to Canada right away. And are we any closer to an understanding of Noah Adler when we are told that he, like all of Richler's heroes, is "cold, insensitive, conscienceless, wantonly destructive of personal relations"? Is this true of the Noah who, when he realizes what has become of his uncle Shloime, is mocked by a whore for the tears which stream down his cheeks? Or the final scene of Noah, when, having demanded and received a Torah from his grandfather, he says, simply, "You have given me what I wanted," and kisses him?

The first requirement of a critic is objectivity. It is not seeing life steadily or whole to suggest that Richler's novels express a dislike of Canada, any more than of Paris, Barcelona or the Finchley Road. And what of the present novel? It is true that, in *A Choice of Enemies*, there is a short scene of a Canadian TV program, "Controversy," which discussed in a rather disreputable way whether Canadian writers must leave the country to develop. It is doubly a pity that Mr. Cohen should think such scenes were proffered as "definitive, basic reasoning." What is definitive and basic in *A Choice of Enemies* does not refer to Canada at all. It concerns the conflict for freedom and survival between a German, Ernst (not, as he reports, Ernest), a stunted gamma-product of defunct ideology, and a Canadian, Norman, who, with all the weaknesses of being undetermined, has the strength of being not-quite-wholly defined. In these important qualities Ernst and Norman are like Kraus and André; again as in *The Acrobats* we see the confrontation of over-articulate Europe and inarticulate America. In both cases, *pace* Mr. Cohen, the highest victory is achieved by the Canadian, even though it is only victory as Conrad saw *Victory*. In general, however, it is misleading to confound the two figures of André and Norman, who differ in age by almost twenty years. André is, for example, young, defiant of category, almost confidently nihilist, ready to punch a stronger, implacable adversary. Norman is almost defeated, only too conscious of the slowly congealing picture of himself, conscious also of a dignity to be preserved, so shy that he brings presents when he goes to call.

A still greater difference between the characters arises from the type of book, the type of world, in which they move and appear. Having succeeded in writing two first novels, Mordecai Richler was too astute to risk a third. André Bennett was a kind of symbol, a symbol to the deprived and unsymbolic world in which he moved and, we suspect, an important symbol to his author as well. We see Norman not as idea, but as reality; he is more puzzled, but less enigmatic. In *The Acrobats*, Richler tended to write from within his characters, all of them; in *A Choice of Enemies* he tends to describe them as they appear and behave. This is a move towards maturity as a writer, even though, as is always the case with maturity, something must be lost.

The change in style is probably no loss. Even in his first book, Richler's style always had a vigorous *presto* movement; but this frequently went underground through galleries of AC-CD nuns and rats floating by in pools of [*sic*] gangrene. It is probably just as well that Richler proved to be not at home in the *monologue intérieur*. The tempo in the newer book is *prestissimo*, the pace being set by sentences like "Horton," "Ernst missed Charlie," "Sally walked." There is no time for free association, only for curt essential memories. The climax is a sequence when Norman goes to tell Vivian he is leaving England, and ends up marrying her instead. It is all over, we are out of the Registry Office, in one and a half pages. This ability to "pack" both event and detail may owe a lot to the skilled blue pencils of commercial writing; but Richler has learned to compress, not by eliminating the small and surprising detail, but by concentrating upon it.

When the crush of event is used to depict motivation, it is quite understandable that we should see characters in a different way. One consequence of this focusing on reality is the emergence into clarity of the minor characters. There is a long Odd-Man-Out parade of these during Norman's period of breakdown and amnesia; some of them, like the woman with the spilly bosom, establish themselves in four or five lines. For this sequence, *The Acrobats* would have attempted only the commonplace of rhapsody; in *A Choice of Enemies* we have the greater eeriness of the world seen as it is, but through a wholly unselective, or differently selective eye.

One cannot, however, depict one's major characters through the technique of thumbnail sketches. In *Son of a Smaller Hero* one had the suspicion that Richler might develop more fully as a portraitist of a group than of an individual. His background seemed to come alive at a glance, while his intuitions of his hero were sometimes incoherent, sometimes unconvincing, sometimes embarrassingly personal. In *A Choice of Enemies*, however, the process of objectification has been almost completed. All of the characters are characters in themselves; no single one of them can be identified as the simple projection of Richler's *propria persona*. Though Norman shares with André and Noah the same kindred search for liberation and for definition, he is in his world only a protagonist, not a microcosm. Other characters reflect each a ray of André's fire: even Sally, who also allows herself to die.

However, in contrast to the facility with which his minor characters fall into view, Richler struggles to create his protagonists with a difficulty which is at once ungainly and arresting. They are, some would say, too important, his motives for creating them too serious, for the down-to-earth medium and style in which he works. Certainly it is true that at times there is a tendency for them to move, not according to their pattern, but to the simpler destiny of Richler's own. At the worst they are manipulated, do not behave but are made to behave, to reach more surely a previously conceived-of conclusion or inconclusion. Charlie Lawson, Karp, Sally, Ernst, even Norman himself, fall into place like pieces of a jig-saw puzzle. This tendency is one which Richler seems to have inherited obliquely from Sartre, his most obvious master: if indulged too far, it could reduce Richler's valid subject to a puppet or peep-show for the idiot-minded. In Sartre the problem is linked to the synthetic nature of existentialist psychology; it is both germane and irremediable. In the case of Richler, whose "philosophy" is eclectic, undisciplined, and tolerant, it is at odds with his deeper gift for accurate vision of diverse people in diverse situations. I would not suggest that the novel is a democracy, and that the author has not the right to order and dismiss his legions at will; but in the exercise of such arbitrary power Richler is still less subtle and skilled than Sartre, more like Arthur Miller, and yet more completely ambitious than Arthur Miller.

Though *A Choice of Enemies* is by far the most finished of Richler's novels, one might, carping, say that it is the least strongly *started*. In *The Acrobats* we had the refreshment of watching an unskilled amateur, knowing none of the ropes, take on the world, and emerge with only the semblance of victory against problems which have never been bested yet. But in Richler's newest book there is indeed a choice of enemies; an established professional, shrewdly aware of his class and weight, is dealing only with manageable problems which seem a little to have been selected in advance. The choice of enemies which Richler states at the end is, like his plot, so wilful, so glib, that we fear we may have been taking him too seriously:

If there was a time to man the barricades, Norman thought, then there is also a time to weed one's private garden. The currency of revolution is invalid as long as both sides bank big bombs. Each age creates its own idiom. This was a time to drop a nickel in the blind man's box and to recommend worth-while movies to strangers, it was a time to play *their* game but to make your *own* errors, a time to wait and a time to hope. The enemy was no longer the boor in power on the right or the bore out of power on the left. All alliances had been discredited. The enemy was the hit-and-run-driver of both sides. . . . So in this time of wrecks, Norman, at the age of thirty-nine, chose at last to lead a private life.

It is the hero who thinks all this, and after the intriguing firmness and hesitancy of his behaviour, his inner confidences (if such these be) are certainly a letdown. Some will find Norman at the book's end a ruined man, or at least someone to be dismissed as nonchalantly as Ernst or Charlie. That would explain the bathos, but it would imply that all Norman has achieved is a separate peace dictated by defeat. I should like to think of this problem in another way.

There are meanwhile other more disturbing features of manipulation and contrivance. What is ostensibly the plot, the contest between one man and another who has (unknown to either) murdered the former's half-brother, has an improbability which fits the Jacobean drama; but in the context of the novel's present conflict it is a thing of no meaning. Ernst, for whose entry so many unlikely scenes and facts have been established, remains a philosophical cipher who fails to win our interest. Punch-lines in conversation, a suspense sequence while Sally dies— these show the trained ignoble hand of an author who, to live, must spend six months a year giving facial surgery to TV scripts. They are faults of a new and serious order. Richler was always an uneven writer, but his earlier blemishes were those of immaturity; these are blemishes of achievement and volition.

If I isolate what I consider to have been faults, it is to protect my claim for the book as a success. It is a success on its own plain-spoken terms, if only because it is contemporary, at a time when so few books are. I cannot understand Mr. Cohen's denial of this most urgent fact. (If *Son of a Smaller Hero* were, as he suggests, related to no real world, it would be an even more remarkable achievement than it is. But that is hardly the complaint that one hears around Montreal. Nor can we accept this charge against the present book, even from the moderator-author of *Fighting Words*.)

Throughout the postwar period we have seen fatigue with ideology and preoccupation with survival. Richler is one of the many authors to have caught this mood: his heroes, those endowed with the most consciousness, want above all to live, and in this book they mostly do. They want to live, not as flattened projections of history or of society, but as individuals grown free of their exhausted roots. To achieve this they must conquer their own hatreds and denials; to do this they must deny their own obsession with themselves. This is the moment of freedom which occurs in all three books, and which allows us to consider them as, if only in Thomas Mann's sense, comedies. *The Acrobats* closes with a symbolic birth, the latest novel with a prosaic but auspicious wedding. Other more fashionable books have already caught this mood of survival, of the new day springing from the field of dragon's teeth. One can cite the endings of works as widely scattered as *Lucky Jim, Look Back in Anger*, and even *The Catcher in the Rye*. Admittedly these three works have not much in common; but in every case their hero stumbles at the end into an affirmation of value that is secure, because it is wholly personal: it is an affirmation, in fact, *against* the society around them. With each work it is possible also to talk of the insufficiency of the ending in terms of the problems posed. We do not feel that anything has *happened* to Jim Dixon or to Jimmy Porter; although we leave them at an opportune moment, we cannot feel that, in future, they will face anything but the old problems and the old boredom. And although the hero of *The Catcher in the Rye* is wholly different, one has the same sense of his isolation *contra mundum*; the same doubt that he will ever change.

Richler's heroes, in contrast, are developed and express themselves, in the larger context of a community; they are not viewers but members, even leaders, of a group. A simple presence of community is in their case only a nostalgic memory: as in Noah's recollections of Prévost (THIS BEACH IS FOR LITVAKS ONLY), and his escape from it, or in Ernst's memories of the *Jungvolk*. They are rather destined to that distinctively twentieth-century condition, the community of the alienated, whose most obvious manifestation is Bohemia. André and Norman are central figures in their Bohemias: their ability to live by their own values is an inspiration or a disturbance to their fellows. But their own need for self-expression is at war with another need, the need to belong. In *A Choice of Enemies*, a preoccupation with the first need leads involuntarily to the satisfaction of the second. The way in which this happens astonishes us; Norman's choice will undoubtedly prove a stumbling-block to many of his contemporaries. But, whatever else, the end of this book should have convinced Mr. Cohen that Richler's heroes are not wholly *révoltés*. They do not really reject their community, but seek to find it as they know it ought to be. Unlike Jimmy Porter, they are stirred to commitment by a memory that Bohemia is not enough.

In this context one must look at Richler's preoccupation with Marxism (or North American Marxism) and the problems of the conscious individual who, because he feels that Marxism has been discredited, sees no way clear towards the attainment of a new social correlative. The postwar sense of loneliness and search for community keeps them also, *faute de mieux*, inside Bohemia. Not the

Bohemia of de Nerval or Wilde, of Bloomsbury and *Art and Letters*—those ruins have not been rebuilt since the war—but their flourishing non-U suburbs of Chelsea Slade students, Cagnes homosexuals, and self-taught artists in Spain. Most American Bohemia has lost its authority: in England it has spread so far as to be scarcely distinguishable. But expatriate Bohemia is important to both continents; and Richler knows how to draw its portrait.

He has also learnt how to catch the mood of a Hampstead pub or shabby bottle party (a red-stained slice of lemon sticking to the bottom of your glass all night). Against this background, Richler sketches a colony of expatriate Canadian scriptwriters, many of them Jewish. The British in the former milieu are polished and sophisticated, but hopeless and dull; together they exhibit the defeated mediocrity of universal secondary education. The Canadians, including Norman, do not have culture as it is known on the Third Programme, but they have preserved their vitality. Most of them, as individuals, are not much; but as a group (due partly to the important factors of their Jewishness and their Marxism) they have a sense of identity which lends itself also to a degree of *panache*. As Sally observes, they share out work in a highly competitive business; they are always lending each other money; an invitation to their parties confers a definite status. To an uncorrupted soul like Vivian out of Fulham, the acquisition of this status seems like a kind of salvation.

Norman knows better. His estrangement, like André's, has gone much farther. He has long ago embraced Noah's experience "that all this time he had only been defining himself Against." Thus his search for liberation is equally a search for definition. Impelled by this search, he has, like all of Richler's heroes, the power of a principled spontaneity. One of Richler's so-called "clichés" is that his heroes are all careless and generous with money. Holden, in *The Catcher in the Rye*, showed the same spontaneous generosity. But it was a generosity of private and momentary significance; Norman, in giving, imposes a certain character upon his environment. The proof that his character has a certain vitality and *envergure* is shown in its effect as example upon others.

The paradox in *A Choice of Enemies* is the apparent sacrifice of this role for another more ordinary and subtle. Norman's character is stripped, in the course of the book, of all its insignia of power, so much so that some reviewers (following Thomas Hale) will see him as a broken man. But Norman's strength was always a matter of weakness. With Sally he could talk about the weakness, but that was all. His relationship with Vivian is of the opposite kind; their intimacy does not dissect these inner problems, but each person has (despite their inability to plan this in a conscious way) acquired a certain value in the life of the other. Certainly there is nothing contrived or *voulu* about Norman's return, like André's, to the simple call of a wife, a child and work. André had an epiphany of engagement; with Norman it is more convincing, an absence, a negative thing. There is a point in the book when we see him wangling an invitation from the crowd he had outgrown, and we realize his heart has been emptied, the affected strength that prevented him has gone. He will allow himself to do the easiest and most difficult thing, to live by accident. And so he marries Vivian; and his fear of his own cowardice, the episode with Hornstein, is seen to have been accepted and conquered.

This note, not of the transcendence but of the survival of disillusion, is what makes Richler so contemporary. I have already quoted from Norman's private existentialism, and suggested that it does not amount to much; but I cannot think that Richler intended the experience to be as barren as the statement. For when we are left with Norman and Vivian, poised on the break of an ordinary day, the book has a humble but haunting power.

What hope, what point there is in Norman's choice, remains inscrutable. Sartre might have closed (as in *Le Diable et le bon Dieu*) with a paradigm, an example of something he has already said very neatly somewhere else. In Richler we must take it upon ourselves to look, not at the statement, but at the situation. *Son of a Smaller Hero* closed with a rather similar, but deliberate, discrepancy between statement (Noah's sullen apology for his independence) and experience (his mother's agony). In that book, though the plot is fatally ambiguous, Noah's certainty of his freedom seems to have been proven wrong. *A Choice of Enemies* closes with an ambiguity not of words, but of situation: in this ambiguity lies Richler's true achievement. Perhaps he is no more sure than in *The Acrobats* of what, on this level, he is trying to say—or even that he is really trying to say anything, for it is so difficult for art to survive when statement begins. I certainly would not wish to impute to him the motives of Tom Thumb fighting to salvage the Western sensibility from individualism. But I do think we can trace in the shape of his writing hitherto the beginning of a powerful and complex insight.

To believe in this insight, one must take Richler's work, as one takes all works of art, partly on its merits, and partly on a kind of faith. ("A suspension of belief and disbelief," croaks the chorus in the marsh: still, what is such a suspension but a kind of faith?) If we ask more for Richler on faith than on demonstration, that is because his novels are less articulate, and to that extent less conscious, than are the novels of any established European. But so are the lives of the Canadians he describes, especially against a European background: his very theme is this conflict of conscious and unconscious. It is a theme we should all respond to in nerve and blood. We have had conscious works of Canadian art. We have had consciously Canadian reviewers. We have also seen some American attempts to set up house in the sub-conscious. In this company we can see one characteristic of Richler's works which Mr. Cohen did not mention: their modesty, their struggle to keep to the experience at hand and to the truth which is available.

THE APPRENTICESHIP OF DISCOVERY

WILLIAM H. NEW

The publication of Mordecai Richler's *The Apprentice-ship of Duddy Kravitz* and Hugh MacLennan's *The Watch that Ends the Night* makes 1959 one of the impor-tant years for recent Canadian fiction. The two works seem at first to be strangely paired. One is a pungently ironic comedy, the other a serious metaphysical study that verges at times on the sentimental. Richler relies on a sprawling picaresque method, and MacLennan on a muted allegory. Even their flaws are different. The tendency to verboseness that afflicts the end of MacLennan's book is nowhere found in Richler's, but Richler will sacrifice the overall balance of his novel for the sake of big comic set scenes. Fortunately his novel survives because his wit is successful, just as MacLennan's work succeeds because the reader becomes sympathetically involved in the reality which the author has created. Yet for all their differences, the two works have the same basic situation. The discovery and habitation of a new land becomes a metaphor for an attitude of mind, and that attitude is at the forefront of present literary thought.

Richler's novel is concerned with the apprenticeship, the voyage, as it were, that ultimately takes Duddy to a new world and gives him the power to create there a recognizable individuality. His childhood position is analogous to that of Jerome Martell in *The Watch that Ends the Night*. While Jerome has known no father, Duddy at the age of fifteen has been unable to find in his

From *Canadian Literature*, No. 29 (Summer 1966); pp. 18-33. By per-mission of the author.

father the qualities he wants to admire, and he invents an extra brother, Bradley, to satisfy this need. While Jerome has not experienced the ordinary expressions of love from his mother, Duddy has not known his mother and is therefore unsure of ever having experienced that love himself. He "couldn't bring himself to risk" asking about this, a key phrase, considering what he will risk, for his incomprehension either of love or of relationship awaits his discovery of an acceptable self. Like Jerome he has a journey to go through part of life, not only inevitable but necessary.

Exactly where the journey should aim and should end is Duddy's problem. When he was only seven, he had been told by his grandfather: "A man without land is nobody. Remember that, Duddel." To find and own land becomes in time, therefore, equated in Duddy's mind with the identity for which he also seeks. But to be a somebody is more than this; to be a somebody is to be adult, not only in the self, but also recognized as being adult by a world to which the self bears some relationship. Maturity does not occur with the discovery of a new world, for this tends not to be a satisfactory end in itself. The dimensions of the new world are greater than the old identity can fill out, and there must be a realistic matching between an individual's potentialities and the place he can occupy. Duddy notes that "South America . . . could no longer be discovered. It had been found." But in reenacting not only the Canadian but also the twentieth-century conflict, he can find a smaller niche elsewhere.

The humour that pervades the book is not gentle, and it serves a quite different purpose from that in, for example, Mitchell's *Who Has Seen the Wind*; there is no necessity here to prevent sentimentality from repelling the reader. Duddy moves through a complicated but essentially extrahuman sequence of events which, because incongruous, excites laughter. The laughter is directed at an outsider to the ordinary human predicament whose conflict is yet typical of it, and because he can surmount his difficulties in unorthodox and cumulatively extravagant ways, he wins, like Donleavy's Ginger Man, a sort of admiration without respect, a sufferance without approval, an attraction without sympathy, and an attachment without involved concern. At once more than the conventional society and an inherent element in it, Duddy follows a course of life in order to locate an appropriate pattern for it. Though this is pursued in iconoclastic—but innocent, and therefore laughable—terms, it illustrates a growth to maturity which is fundamentally parallel to the serious situations involving MacLennan's George Stewart. The changes that take place in Duddy prepare him for the discovery of Lac St. Pierre, and the discovery is an essential step in his growing up.

Duddy is a comer; he pushes his way to success not by having any idea of a reasonable means to do this, but rather by not having any idea and so using every means as though it were a reasonable one. The losses he incurs in a crooked roulette game stem from his naiveté, and they recall his earlier loss of a much smaller capital invested in a stock of obscene comic books. His earlier reaction had been to burn the stock for fear of being caught with it; the reaction at Ste. Agathe is to run away; yet both are childish in a way that Duddy cannot be if he is to emerge from his apprenticeship in his own terms. The novel has its limited success because the reader will let Duddy have those terms; they reverse standard values, but they become values in themselves.

Because he is a comic figure, a sort of latter-day *picaron* seeking ruthlessly and ultimately successfully for social promotion, Richler must not cultivate for him the reader's pity. If there were a total identification between the reader and the central character, the comic effect would be destroyed, for it is the sense of apartness, of differentiation between the character perceived and the concept the reader has of himself, that is part of the ironic comedy. Duddy, that is, must remain innocent even in success, even though he moves through his failures to a triumph that he does not fully comprehend. The identity that he finally achieves, successful in spite of its disergard for social convention, is both typical of the society he has been scorning and yet beyond it. The "maturity" he reaches by the end of his apprenticeship is a recognition of a place in relation to society that will probably through time generate social acceptance as well; at that time, perhaps, reader and character could move closer together, but not until. His solution is distinct, then, from that found within a social code by George Stewart, though it is related to the individual one formulated by Jerome Martell.

Duddy's childishness concerning the comics and the roulette must be avoided not because it is socially irresponsible but because it does not contribute to the self for which he aims. Because he has been reared in the St. Urbain Street world of Montreal, a sort of Jewish enclave of low average income, he has been brought up to expect defensive protection as necessary. Several choices are open to him as routes to success: immersion in the Gentile world with concomitant loss of identity, continuation of the St. Urbain Street world of his childhood, participation in the establishment of the new Jewish state of Israel, or the achievement of an independence that will let him be himself in any situation. An attempt to achieve independence, however, makes Duddy uneasy and suspicious because he is insecure. The very defences that protect against any envelopment by the "alien" culture preserve the St. Urbain Street childhood identity as well. Duddy's brother Lennie removes those defences in his contact with the Westmount Gentiles, but that society only consumes him. He thinks he finds there a freedom that his own deliberate childhood existence did not supply: "They're just themselves and glad of it. Nothing scares them. . . . *They're young.*" But Duddy voices the truth later when he says: "It's hard to be a gentleman—a Jew, I mean—it's hard to be. Period."

To achieve independence in the Gentile world, Duddy assumes he needs money. When he was a child, the identity he had wanted was bound up with his appraisal of Jerry Dingleman, the Boy Wonder, the Mr. Big of a narcotics underworld. "Duddy wanted to be a somebody. Another Boy Wonder maybe. Not a loser, certainly." But the Boy Wonder is exactly that, a *boy* wonder, because in spite of his power in a localized area and in spite of his wealth, he does not achieve recogntion by the Westmount world. Before Duddy recognizes that the Wonder is "only famous on St. Urbain Street," he is used, unaware, to smuggle heroin. Dingleman says of him: "The boy is innocent. He's perfect." The innocence that Dingleman sees in Duddy is a naiveté perfect for being exploited. Because the boy seeks to masquerade in an imagined sophistication he will avoid questioning what he does not understand, when questioning would be the very act that would bring him real knowledge. To come out of apprenticeship, Duddy needs not only to discover truth in the world in which he wants to live but also to know what to do with truth. Dingleman can be defeated not by confronting him with fact (which he has known and disregarded all along) but only by an independence that can afford to disregard him. Duddy's various schemes for achieving the wealth to purchase Lac St. Pierre give him a measure of the experience he needs to be independent of Dingleman; what he needs also, in the way of position achieved through a recognition by self and by others, he has yet to find out.

Duddy must both extend trust and be extended trust before he can achieve recognizable adult status. For this to be part of any development in him in Richler's comic terms as well, it must be his extension of trust that brings him knowledge of the nature of this relationship but the extension of trust to him that in fact brings with it the success that is maturity and mastery. Duddy's grandfather,

Simcha, is an adult of the old order; he merits trust in his neighbourhood and is given it, and it is a measure of his position. But for Duddy the estimation of that world is insufficient, and though one of his plans in securing Lac St. Pierre is to please his grandfather, this must ultimately give way to the more basic need to fulfill himself. He cannot live in Simcha's world; no more can Simcha live in his. The final recognition of their separate identities is prefigured when early in the novel Abromovitch says to his father "This is modern times."

When Duddy trusts others, his comic naiveté takes him into situations that more experienced persons would avoid, but it is simply because he is naive that he can emerge unscathed, though more knowing, developing cunning in the process. He lets Dingleman use him for smuggling heroin, for example; he unknowingly lets Peter John Friar make *avant garde* films of a *bar mitzvah* ceremony for him; he purchases Lac St. Pierre in Yvette's name, saying, "A friend is a friend. You've got to trust somebody. . . ." But it is his central and significant relationship with his brother that the difference between intelligent trust and foolhardiness crystallizes for him, that he learns he must make a choice of enemies. Lennie had tried to become part of Westmount society and in so doing was gulled into foolhardy action; he is a promising medical student, and yet he jeopardizes his career by performing—and botching—an illegal abortion, and then running away childishly, to hide from the act. Duddy, however, can not only diagnose the cause but also prescribe the cure: "Don't you know better than to go bareback?" If mature life is a healthy self-possession, then the life lived prior to maturity must be based on self-protection. When Duddy then takes Lennie's problem from him and solves it, earning Lennie's trust, he has achieved part of the relationship that will ultimately give him his final position. Lennie finds his own identity by breaking with Westmount and participating in the building of Israel, by taking his doctor's capacity for healing to a new world that he can inhabit; but Duddy's place remains in the Gentile world. His is therefore different from Cohen, who says: "We're two of a kind, you know. . . . A plague on all the *goyim*, that's my motto." He is different because, for Duddy, this is not a satisfactory guide; he cannot choose to align himself on religious terms. When his film of Bernie Cohen's *bar mitzvah* shows "the pregnant moment, the meeting of time past and time present, when the priest and his initiate read the *ho'mat*," and shows it, in a hilariously funny scene, by techniques of symbolism and montage, the orthodox apprenticeship to position within the religion is contrasted with Duddy's unorthodox but vigorous apprenticeship to an identity all his own.

Though the story is related in terms of a Jewish boy's rise to adult status, its implications go beyond the strictly racial-religious extension. Duddy's Uncle Benjy is wrong when his estimation of the boy begins and ends here: "Because you're a *pusherke*. A little Jew-boy on the make." What Duddy comes to and in fact must come to if his apprenticeship to life is to be successful is *a* self rather than *the* self. He cannot accept an order that is established for him by race or religion or duty or family, and when Benjy leaves him a letter—which Duddy must be ready to read, somewhat like Nick Adams or Ike McCaslin having to be ready to fish or hunt—the warning it contains to the boy must even yet undergo seachange within him before he can become a man: "You've got to love [the family], Duddel. . . . A boy can be two, three, four potential people, but a man is only one. He murders the other." The relationship of family love is only valid for him up to a point. Inheritance of family ties—in individual or even in political terms, for the "ghetto," for Montreal, and for the Canadian society of the story—must not interfere with the establishment of individual identity. Lennie and Riva find their "God's Little Acre" in Israel but, though this satisfies them, it cannot become *ergo* a necessary reason for Duddy's embracing the same solution. His own little acres lies at Lac St. Pierre, neither in Israel nor in St. Urbain Street, and love that enmeshes him elsewhere than in that self deprives him of his full potentialities and ends by being no love.

He has to become a Somebody, and for this to occur, the demanding love that had attempted to form the child's identity must be exchanged for a trust in the identity that the adult forms for himself. Lennie has to trust Duddy in the matter of the abortion; Max has to trust him with a thousand dollar loan; Benjy has to show his trust by willing Duddy his house. Duddy's particular personality causes a change when the comic reversal of intent takes place; not only does he avoid all other selves in his mastery of one, but he also turns to his own development the trusts that are placed in him by others. The abortion affair leads to his business ventures with Hugh Calder of Westmount, for example; the house that Benjy leaves him, tied up as it is by legal limitations so that Duddy can only own the legacy and not profit in his own cash terms by it, he empties of its furniture in order to raise money anyway and invest it in the acquisition of his own land. What Yvette will not willingly give him is the opportunity ultimately to be adult; she wants a cessation of imaginative investment and practical energy which is objectified in her care for the paralytic Virgil. Whereas Duddy finds himself by expending, Virgil remains fearful and in need of protection by trying to save intact a bequest that has been left to him. When Duddy sacrifices that tradition to his own effort, he brings the traditional world—albeit weak and by now impotent: Simcha, Dingleman, Virgil— into opposition against him. But when he is recognized as the Owner of the new world, his apprenticeship of discovery is over. He is given a trust that makes him at last the Somebody he wants to be ("That's all right, sir. We'll mark it.") adult, individual, and master in his own terms in his own land.

Success is therefore possible in Richler's fictional world, though his ironic eye builds it only out of breaking traditions. This seems at first to be so partial as to deny adequate scope to the novel, and in Richler's other works this is essentially true. The acrimony of *The Incomparable Atuk,* for example, makes that work merely repellent instead of provocative. *A Choice of Enemies* and *Son of a Smaller Hero* offer only fragmentary views of society, and hence the reader never quite believes in their reality. But the world of Duddy Kravitz is whole, and Duddy himself, while not particularly likeable, is very much alive. He wins readers to his side, moreover, because his reaction to traditions is a positive one. The control he wants, the mastery to which he is apprenticed, is a valid aim. His iconoclasm is of value not for itself, but because it is a route towards inhabiting a new world and fulfilling a social individuality. As he is a comic figure, his apparently destructive tendencies can paradoxically be a means for constructing life, but the fictional tone and technique are necessarily different for depicting this than they are for showing a comparable process of discovery in *The Watch that Ends the Night.* MacLennan's study is of the crossing of political and metaphysical frontiers and it ends in peace, whereas Richler's novel, of a different kind, ends in a comic triumph. . . .

WOLF IN THE SNOW

The House Repossessed

WARREN TALLMAN

. . . Along St. Urbain street in Montreal, the marvellous, the splendid and the amazing have given way to the commonplace, the shabby and the unspeakable. And even before thinking of anything so portentous as a new self, Mordecai Richler has been engaged in the much more onerous task of clearing away the debris which has accumulated in a world where all disguises have been put in doubt. His first three novels are studies of ruined lives: André, the guilt-haunted Canadian artist, who is eventually murdered by the Nazi Kraus, whose sister Theresa then commits suicide; the guilt-ridden homosexual, Derek, his equally guilty sister, Jessie, and her equally guilty husband, the alcoholic Barney; the Wellington College professor Theo Hall and his wife, Miriam; Norman, the American Fifth Amendment expatriate whose brother is murdered by Ernst, the German youth whom Sally, the Toronto girl, ruins her life trying to save. All of these persons reach out, cry out, for any masks other than the ones they have.

And they testify to Richler's affinity with that side of modern life where the misbegotten wander through ruined Spains of self-pity, poisoned to the point of near and at times actual madness by self-loathing. However, Richler does not seek out these persons in order to demonstrate several times over that we are wrapped up like so many sweating sardines in world misery, world guilt, world sorrow. Like André, Norman and Noah, the protaganists

From *Canadian Literature*, No. 6 (Autumn 1960); pp. 41-48. By permission of the author.

of these novels, he is inside the misery looking for a way out. What looks out is a courageous intelligence struggling to realize that the tormented sleep of self loathing which he explores is just that—a sleep, a dream, a nightmare: but not the reality.

In his fourth novel, *The Apprenticeship of Duddy Kravitz,* the sleeper begins to come awake. The nightmare is still there, but it is not the same nightmare. In *The Acrobats* and *A Choice of Enemies,* Richler chooses areas of world guilt as the basis for dream terror. The Spanish war, the second world war, the victims of these wars and of their ideologies make up the manifest content, the general human failure which images and invites the latent personal failures represented. People whose lives have gone smash drift into areas where life has gone smash and consort with the ghosts who have survived. In *Duddy Kravitz* the scope contracts. Both the ghosts who make up the nightmare and the ideologies through which they wander have faded from mind. Duddy's father, his brother Lenny, his uncle and aunt, his teacher MacPherson, his friend Virgil, his enemy Dingleman and his shiksa Yvette all live tangled lives in a world where they do not know themselves. But they are caught up by personal disorders rather than world disorder, family strife rather than international strife, individual conflict rather than ideological conflict. And within the localized dream we meet an entirely different dreamer. We meet the direct intelligence and colloquial exuberance that is Duddy's style—and Richler's.

T. S. Eliot has said that poetry in our time is a mug's game. So is fiction, and Richler is one of the mugs. Duddy has ceased to care for appearances and this insouciance releases him from the nightmare. All of the other people in the novel cannot possess themselves because their vital energies are devoted full-time to maintaining the false appearances in terms of which they identify themselves. These appearances—the cultural, ethical, communal pretensions to which they cling—mask over but scarcely conceal the distinctly uncultured, unethical, isolated actuality in which they participate. Hence the importance in their lives of Dingleman, the Boy Wonder, who is a projection of their actual longings to be at ease in Zion in a Cadillac at the same time as he is a projection of the limitation of these longings, being hopelessly crippled. But Duddy, who has ceased to care for appearances, sees people for what they are, himself included. And what he sees, he accepts— himself included. In an acquisitive world he is exuberantly acquisitive. When he is tricked, he weeps. When threatened, he becomes dangerous. When attacked, he bites back. When befriended, he is generous. When hard-pressed he becomes frantic. When denied, he is filled with wrath. From the weave of this erratic shuttling, a self struggles into presence, a naive yet shrewd latter-day Huck Finn, floating on a battered money raft down a sleazy neon river through a drift of lives, wanting to light out for somewhere, wanting somewhere to light out for.

Plato tells us that when a new music is heard the walls of the city tremble. The music in Duddy Kravitz is where in novels it always is, in the style. The groove in which the style runs is that of exuberance, shifting into exaggeration, shifting into those distortions by which Richler achieves his comic vision of Montreal. The finest parts of the novel are those in which Richler most freely indulges the distortions: the sequence in which the documentary film director Friar produces a wedding ceremony masterpiece which views like the stream of consciousness of a lunatic, a fantasia of the contemporary mind; the entire portrait of Virgil who wants to organize the epileptics of the world and be "their Sister Kenny," as well as the more sombre portraits of Dingleman and Duddy's aunt Ida. Because Duddy has ceased to care for appearances, he moves past all of the genteel surfaces of the city and encounters an actuality in which all that is characteristically human has retreated to small corners of conscious-

ness, and life becomes a grotesque game played by be-
wildered grotesques. The persons who make up this gallery
not only fail to invoke self but can scarcely recognize what
it is to be a human being. They are like uncertain creatures in a fabulous but confusing zoo, not sure why they
are there, not even sure what human forest they once
inhabited.

They testify in the language of the sometimes comic,
sometimes grim, distortions Richler has created to the
oppressive weight of doubt, guilt, remorse, shame and
regret that history has imposed upon modern man, particularly upon man in the city, where the effects of history,
most closely organized, are most acutely felt. The greater
the system of threats to self, the more extensive the system
of appearances needed to ward off those threats, the more
marked the distortions of characteristic human need and
desire. And the more marked the distortions, the more
difficult the artist's task. For sensibility, that active sum of
the artist's self, never does exist in relation to itself alone.
It exists in relation to what *is*—actual persons, an actual
city, actual lives. When the impact of accomplished history
imposes distortions upon that actuality, sensibility must
adjust itself to the distortions. The story of these adjust-
ments is, I think, the most significant feature of North
American fiction in our time. Long ago and far away,
before World War One o'clock, Theodore Dreiser could
look at the world with direct eyes. Characteristic human
impulses of love, sorrow, hope, fear, existed in the actual
world as love, sorrow, hope, fear; and Dreiser could direct
his powerful sensibility into representation which was, as
they say, "like life." But after World War One, in *The
Great Gatsby,* possibly the most significant of the between-
wars novels, there is open recognition of a distorted
actuality necessitating a reordering of sensibility, one
which both Gatsby and Fitzgerald fail to achieve.

Since World War Two the need for adjustment has become even more marked, simply because the distortions

have become more pronounced. In *Duddy Kravitz,* Richler follows closely in the groove of Duddy's exuberance and on out into the exaggerations and distortions which make up his adjustment to actual Montreal. By doing so he is able to achieve an authentic relationship to life in that city—Duddy's dream of Caliban along the drear streets of Zoo. In this Richler is at one with the considerable group of contemporary writers—call them mugs, call them angry, call them beat—who all are seeking in their art those readjustments which will permit them to relate their sensibilities to what actually is. History has had and continues to have her say. These writers are trying to answer back. If the vision which Richler achieves in answer to history jars upon our sensibilities, that is because we have all heard of Prospero's cloud-capped towers and gorgeous palaces. Yet, if the style which conveys the vision twangles from glib to brash, from colloquial to obscene, that is because the true North American tone, at long past World War Two o'clock, is much closer to that of Caliban than ever it has been to that of Prospero whose magic was a European magic, long sunk from sight. and whose daughter and her beau and their world are out of fashion like old tunes or like the lovers on Keats' urn, maybe forever but address unknown. The brave new world toward which Duddy's self quickens is the lake property he covets throughout the novel and finally possesses. When he dives in, seeking a rebirth, he scrapes bottom. But he doesn't care, he doesn't care, he doesn't care. Which is why the mug can make with the music.

D. H. Lawrence contended that in the visions of art a relatively finer vision is substituted for the relatively cruder visions extant. But in North Amerca, as I hope this restricted study at least partially confirms, finer is relatively crude, because frequently untrue, and crude can be relatively fine. All too often, in fiction as in life, those pretensions which we seek out because they make us fine provide false furnishings for the actual house in which we live. This fine is crude. Duddy, who would not know a pretension if he met one, wanders for this reason by accident and mostly unaware into the actual house. His crude is relatively fine. True, there are no gods hovering over Duddy's lake, no grandiose hotel, no summer camp for children. There is only old mother North America with her snow hair, her mountain forehead, her prairie eyes, and her wolf teeth, her wind songs and her vague head of old Indian memories. And what has she to do with Duddy Kravitz? A lot, I think. For when the house is repossessed the gods come back—snow gods, dust gods, wind gods, wolf gods—but life gods too. And life is the value. When history conspires against life, ruining the house, life will fight back in the only way it can, by not caring. Heavy, heavy doesn't hang over Duddy's head. And that is his value.

Snow melts away. Mountains can be very beautiful. Wheat is growing on the prairies. And in the dark forest beside the hidden lakes the deer are standing, waiting. So turn off the neon, tune out the noise, and place Duddy in the foreground of the scene. . . .

THE APPRENTICESHIP OF DUDDY KRAVITZ

A. R. BEVAN

At first glance, Mordecai Richler's novel seems to fit into the tradition of Joyce's *Portrait of the Artist* and Lawrence's *Sons and Lovers*, each of which deals with the growing up of a young man to the point where he is on his own, alone and lonely, ready to strike out in life freed from the ties of his youth. Stephen Dedalus deliberately separates himself from Ireland and all it stands for in order to become a writer: "To forge in the smithy of my soul the uncreated conscience of my race." His solitary condition is the result of long thought and much self-examination; he has made a choice and has consciously accepted the responsibility for his own life. The reader shares with him some of his elation, some of his excitement, the novel ending as an affirmation of man's creative spirit. Lawrence's hero, Paul Morel, turns at the end of the novel back towards the lights of the city, walking quickly away from the darkness that had embraced his dead mother: "He would not take that direction, to the darkness, to follow her. He walked towards the faintly humming, glowing town, quickly." Again we are made to feel as the novel ends that the young man has made a choice, has re-entered the world of life and vitality. In both of these earlier novels the protagonist has made a choice of direction, aware of the chain of events that had made such a choice possible and necessary. Each has made a decision, based on thought and self-awareness, and each has chosen a way

The introduction to *The Apprenticeship of Duddy Kravitz*; New Canadian Library, McClelland & Stewart Ltd., Toronto, 1969. By permission of McClelland & Stewart.

of life that is an affirmation of man's greatness or potential greatness.

Richler's novel, however, in spite of its superficial affinity with the two novels mentioned above, ends with no such affirmation. His protagonist, who has never weighed the consequences of his actions in any but material terms, is less alone in the physical sense than the earlier young men, but he is also much less of a man. His decisions have been made on the wrong terms, have been based on nothing at all. He has destroyed himself and others for a piece of land that means nothing to those who have loved him. He has devoted his energy to acquiring property; he has done nothing to develop himself. Whereas the other two, Stephen Dedalus and Paul Morel, have matured, and have decided the course of their lives for themselves, poor Duddy has simply gone along without realizing where he was headed. He is a modern "anti-hero" (something like the protagonist in Anthony Burgess's *A Clockwork Orange*) who lives in a largely deterministic world, a world where decisions are not decisions and where choice is not really choice.

In another sense Duddy reminds us (at least he reminds me) of Tom Jones the foundling. Duddy has no mother and not much of a father; he asks all his relatives about his mother but never actually finds out if she had ever loved him. He is almost as much an orphan as Tom Jones, and like Tom he sets out to find his place in the world. Moreover, Duddy's search for himself has strongly picaresque overtones; like Tom he ranges through a very broad spectrum of his society, exposing to the reader the vices and follies of the world in which he is forced to make his way. He is less fortunate than Tom, for whom everything works out beautifully, since Duddy discovers at the end of the novel that he belongs to the world of Max and Eddy and Jerry Dingleman. He learns that there is no place for him in the gentle, loving and kindly world of his grandfather, or even in the world of Yvette and Virgil. His

frantic headlong search ends with his discovery that he fits
all too well into a vulgar and raucous world devoid of
understanding and love. If we take Duddy seriously as a
character, and I think we should, the novel ends on a very
sad note.

Duddy Kravitz, obsessed with the land he eventually is
successful in acquiring, is destroyed by following an assortment of false gods he picks up at random from all sorts of
people in his life. Like a parrot, he hears and then adopts
phrases and ideas that no doubt have had some special
significance to the people who first used them, but to
Duddy they have become not much more than verbal
bromides. He uncritically swallows and later throws out
as his own such undigested gems as Lennie's "Anatomy is
the big killer," and Cohen's "There's not a businessman in
town who hasn't at least one bankruptcy in his pocket,"
and most important of all his grandfather's "A man without land is nobody." It is this last speech that directs
Duddy's actions throughout the novel. Ironically, it is the
comment of Simcha Kravitz, the chief representative in
the novel of the old lost world of solid virtues and sound
values, that turns his grandson into a person possessed of
a materialistic demon. Duddy becomes a ruthless entre-
preneur with an impressive list of sins of omission and
commission to his discredit, and all to follow the dream
implanted in him by the kindly old Simcha.

Duddy gets his land; but, because he believes that any
means can be justified by the beauty of his vision of the
future, he emerges at the end of the novel as a failure in
all the relationships that should have mattered to him. He
is rejected by his grandfather, and by Yvette and Virgil,
and is left with the loud unthinking admiration of his
father, Max the Hack. (We agree with Uncle Benjy that
"Max is not very bright.") The people Duddy admires
have come to see him for what he is, whereas those who
have learned to admire him see only what he has accomplished. Max knows nothing about the conniving tricks;

the others do. When Duddy tells himself that "I'm going to get that land no matter what, see?" he expresses to himself much the same idea as the earlier accusation of his brother Lennie, "What's in it for me, that's your philosophy."

It is difficult to feel very much sympathy for Duddy until perhaps the end of the novel; he is just too aware of the enormity of his own actions to pass for an innocent, and he causes the destruction of too many people to be seen only as a victim of his unfortunate environment. From one point of view we are presented to Duddy as a poor little neglected underprivileged boy from the slums and therefore one who cannot be blamed for trying to improve his lot even by slippery tactics. But the Duddy that we usually see is the one described as "a cretinous little money-grubber," as "a little Jew-boy on the make," as "a busy, conniving little Yid," and as a "scheming little bastard." It is true that his Uncle Benjy, who is one of the "lousy intelligent people!" (to use Duddy's description of him), realizes just before his own death that there might be something else about his nephew: "You're two people . . . The scheming little bastard I saw so easily and the fine intelligent boy underneath that your grandfather, bless him, saw." He goes on to tell Duddy that "a boy can be two, three, four potential people, but a man is only one. He murders the others." Richler obviously presents Uncle Benjy as one of the spokesmen for the minority view, a sort of chorus figure commenting on the central character and indirectly on society at large. We are prepared by the author to accept Uncle Benjy's reading of Duddy's character and we see Duddy as he saw him, and at the end of the novel we see that all the other potential people present in the boy have been murdered by the scheming little bastard. He has become another Boy Wonder!

The original Boy Wonder, Jerry Dingleman, is an important character in the novel. As Max describes the exploits of the Boy Wonder in words and tone suited to an epic hero, Dingleman the racketeer becomes to Duddy the living symbol of success. He has money, power and girls, and he made it all himself: "And from what? Streetcar transfers at three cents apiece. Streetcar transfers, that's all. I mean can you beat that?" Not even Duddy can, but he tries hard. When we actually meet the Boy Wonder as presented directly by Richler and not through the gullible eyes of Max, we immediately recognize him as an unscrupulous, predatory, and successful crook. His physical appearance, changed greatly for the worse by his "personal troubles" (polio), is to the reader clearly indicative of his moral corruption, another personal trouble that has had at least as much effect upon the impression he makes upon others. It takes poor Duddy a long, long time to recognize his hero for what he really is, a "two-bit, dope-smuggling cripple." Max, it is interesting to note, continues in his admiration of Dingleman, and his highest praise of Duddy is to see his son in the same way. In the last paragraph of the novel, after Duddy has been rejected by Simcha, Yvette and Virgil, he returns to the admiration of Max, apparently accepting it as the real, the genuine, the true evaluation of his achievement: "And suddenly Duddy did smile. He laughed. He grabbed Max, hugged him, and spun him around. 'You see,' he said, his voice filled with marvel. 'You see.' " His triumph is on the scale of values set up by the Boy Wonder, whose greatest advocate is the not-very-bright Max the Hack.

The novel ends then as a devastating attack on the world of Duddy Kravitz, which is the world of Jewish Montreal. It is interesting to note that Duddy's Montreal is a bicultural city, Jewish and non-Jewish. All non-Jews, French and English, are seen as pretty much the same; the two-culture theme of *Two Solitudes* takes on a new look in Richler's novel. He is obviously very aware of the flaws in his own society, and on one plane the novel is a bitter revelation of the vulgarity and raw materialism of middle-class Canadian life, for Richler well exemplified by the world he still probably knows best. There are a few admirable Jews presented very briefly and used to reveal even more clearly by contrast the glittering false standards of the many; but for the most part Richler emphasizes all too strongly the aspects of Jewish society that the anti-Semites do. The few warm and unselfish characters we meet remain largely undeveloped and lifeless: Simcha the representative of the old world; Hersh, the only student at school who openly criticizes Duddy's destruction of MacPherson, the alcoholic teacher whose invalid wife dies answering one of Duddy's anonymous and scurrilous phone calls; Bernie Altman, the one fellow-waiter not dedicated to ridiculing the outsider; perhaps Yvette, Duddy's Girl Friday; and Virgil, the epileptic ruthlessly used by Duddy. But it is not only the sympathetic characters who fail to come to life; we also get to know very little about any character other than Duddy himself. Other characters are seen only in terms of their relationship with Duddy, whose apprenticeship is the subject of the novel. There are brilliant sketches of many minor characters, such as Auntie Ida, Cuckoo Kaplan, Rabbi Goldstone and many others, but they remain as extras.

Duddy and his development as a full-fledged member of his world occupy the centre of the stage at all times. And we do have a chance to know him. At least we see him in action, and we are allowed to enter his mind and to see what his motives are and what he wants to do with his life. Unfortunately for Duddy he doesn't always know himself very well, not well enough to see that he is consistently following the wrong set of values, even though these are the accepted values of the world in which he lives. Max, proudly reminiscing about his highly successful son, gives praise for the wrong acts: "You could see from the day of his birth that he was slated for fame and fortune. A comer. Why I remember when he was still at F.F.H.S. they had a teacher there, an anti-Semite of the anti-Semites, a lush-head, and my boy was the one who led the fight against him and drove him out of the school." Of course, Duddy does know himself better than Max knows him, and he does have some uneasy thoughts about his share in the ruin of the kindly MacPherson and even wonders if he did somehow kill Mrs. MacPherson by accident by phoning when old Mac was not at home. It is in Duddy's occasional moments of self-examination that the reader develops some sympathy for the kid "born on the wrong side of the tracks with a rusty spoon in his mouth, so to speak, and the spark of rebellion in him."

Canadian novelists seem to me to be a very conventional lot, at least as far as experiments with form go (*The Double Hook* stands out for me as the shining exception to the rule), and certainly in this novel Richler is a traditionalist. We do have a short break in the generally straightforward chronology when, after meeting Duddy as a particularly nasty, fifteen-year old schoolboy, we go back to learn something about his earlier exploits, and especially about his relationship with his grandfather, a relationship that gave the old man's friends cause to worry: "The round-shouldered old men looked at Duddy and decided he was mean, a crafty boy, and they hoped he would not hurt Simcha too hard." Then we move back to Duddy at seventeen and carry on from there. There is no playing with any experimental form here either. We see everything as Duddy sees it, but not through any stream-of-consciousness; Duddy is always fully conscious, and with only minor excursions into his dream world we follow all the action as Duddy scurries from job to job, from deal to deal, from scrape to scrape. In the narrative and descriptive sections of the novel Richler writes good, sound, correct English, perhaps a bit too much like a good term essay. It seems to me that Richler handles dialogue exceptionally well, giving us conversations of great range and convincing authenticity: Duddy and his schoolmates with their smutty and suggestive comments on life and love; the loud, vulgar, and raucous remarks on the film HAPPY BAR-

MITZAH, BERNIE!; the talk of Max and his mates; the maudlin psychological jargon of Auntie Ida; and many others. The book comes to life through its dialogue, and the vitality of dialogue is usually a reliable test of the success of a novel.

There is always a temptation to evaluate Canadian writers by comparison with other Canadians. Written by a Canadian and about Canadians in Canada's largest city, this novel with its satiric-tragic-comic attitude to man in the modern world is much more than a "mere" Canadian work. Richler's novel, it seems to me, can stand on its own by any standard.

MORDECAI RICHLER

Craftsman or Artist

NAIM KATTAN

In an article which he wrote for the special number that the American travel magazine *Holiday* recently devoted to Canada, Mordecai Richler said:

Finally, the best influences in the world reach us from New York. The longest unmanned frontier in the world is an artificial one and I look forward to the day when it will disappear and Canadians will join fully in the American adventure. To say this in Canada is still to invite cat-calls and rotten eggs. We would lose our identity, they say, our independence. But Texas or Maine still have distinctive identities and we are even now economically dependent on the United States.

This is the logical conclusion that can be glimpsed behind Mordecai Richler's whole literary output and behind the intellectual and psychological processes from which it springs. Before accepting the argument of the cultural supremacy of the United States, this Canadian novelist explored all the ways which might have led him to a vigorous affirmation of the cultural autonomy of Canada.

The journey of Mordecai Richler in fact runs along two parallel lines which are actually projections of the same hunger and the same will to succeed; he is an adolescent doubling as the child of an immigrant.

This immigrant's son was born at a time when a middle class was beginning to take shape in the heart of the Jewish

From *Canadian Literature*, No. 21 (Summer 1964); pp. 46-51. Translated from the French by George Woodcock. Reprinted by permission of the author and the translator.

community. The child who first saw the light in the old Jewish quarter of Montreal shared the dreams and hopes of a generation which was born in Canada and wished to gather with both hands the possibilities of that American land. For that purpose, it was necessary for him to detach himself from his family, from his group, from his quarter. How could this be done when the family and the quarter, the traditions of the group and the customs of the household, were inextricably mingled together?

In such circumstances the young man chose to reject them all at the same time. He had neither the determination nor the intellectual power to disentangle the overt and the hidden forces which formed the texture of the collective life in which he had been forced to participate. He therefore chose, as his first step, escape.

His hostility to Canadian provincialism was accentuated by the presence of a provincialism which seemed to him even narrower and which gripped him like an iron halter— that of the family. To affirm himself, he must prove himself not merely as an adult, but also as a man open to all the widest horizons of the universe. He therefore departed from Canada. The ancestral land was neither his destination nor his first port of call. Following the steps of the Lost Generation, this young pilgrim wished to demonstrate that the world in all its breadth belonged to him. Breathing the smoke-laden air of the bars of France and Spain, he thought in this way to pose his candidature for inclusion in the great company of powerful and adventurous writers. But in imagining that he was following in the steps of Hemingway, Richler deceived himself, for he was merely reviving once again and in a more complicated manner the adventures of a past decade described by Bud Schulberg in *What makes Sammy Run?*

At the age of 22, Richler's first novel, *The Acrobats,* brought to light one of the richest promises in the young tradition of Canadian literature. *The Acrobats* is in itself a mediocre novel, but, though it has all the pretentiousness and all the imperfections of a beginner's work, it reveals qualities which could equally well be those of a clever craftsman or those of a true writer.

Richler uses every means to avoid speaking directly of Canada and particularly of Canadian Jews. He sets his stage as far as possible from St. Urbain Street—in Valencia, in Spain. The complex intrigues, fruits of a fevered imagination, hide imperfectly the real anxieties of the young novelist. Since timidity and bashfulness prevent him from speaking in the first person, Richler disguises his characters to the best of his ability, clothing them in borrowed garments which barely hide the conventional faces of the wicked who succeed and the good who are defeated.

His Canadian hero is not Jewish. He is an English-speaking painter who wishes to mingle with Jews but merely succeeds in making pregnant a daughter of Israel who dies from an attempted abortion. The real Jew is a bar-keeper, a gentle and corrupted American, generous and unscrupulous, who has lost his bearings and, despite all Richler's efforts, does not emerge as a cynic.

In his second novel, *Son of a Smaller Hero,* the masks fall away. Richler does not speak in the first person, but the autobiographical tone of the book is not entirely deceptive. It is the world of his own childhood that he reveals in fictional form. The adolescent hero deprived of childhood takes his revenge. He sits in judgement on a family which has cut him off too early from an affection he desperately demanded. Three generations face each other: the adolescent Noah, romantic, sentimental, ambitious; Wolf, the father, the false hero; and the grandfather Melech, the patriarch, the guardian of the treasure handed on from generation to generation. The symbolism of the novel is too easily unravelled not to make mention of it. Wolf passes for a hero because he saves from the fire a box which everyone believes contains the rolls of the Torah but which, in his mind, only contains money. Noah is therefore right to rebel against parents who exploit authentic traditions merely to distort them, to empty them of content and meaning. Fortunately the grandfather is there to remind one that this religion which his unscrupulous children have debased had once, in an age now departed, a truth that has since been obscured and concealed.

The adolescent cannot cross the frontiers of the ghetto without doing violence to himself. He is too much affected by the traditions which nourished his childhood for him to be able to reject them except by force. It would be treating this rage of youth too seriously if we were to elevate Richler into the censor and critic of a whole community.

It is to his family that the hero owes a grudge; it is his family he accuses of not bearing the same love and feeling as he does toward a doctrine which he would like to maintain in its pristine purity, that is to say, without modification by the demanding laws of existence.

This is clearly the mental process of the adolescent. And this is what gives the novel movement, if not power. The ambitious youth who has made his reckoning with a narrow society is propelled by an irrepressible impulse. He wishes to deal as a man with adult problems. After all, has he not set himself free? Has he not said what he thinks of those who do not see beyond the wall of the ghetto? Now he must face them with the proofs of his initiation into manhood.

In *A Choice of Enemies* the ghetto, instead of vanishing, gains ground. The young Canadian leaves his country in search of horizons as wide as his ambitions. He is Canadian, and it is as a Canadian that he wishes to affirm himself. New York? It is too near, and too much like home; he would be drowned there in the mass of thousands of immigrants' sons who hope to devour ravenously the fruits promised by a powerful and prosperous America. In

London this subject of the Commonwealth feels that he might not be lost as he would be in a North America that refuses to take his Canadian characteristics seriously. But in the metropolis of the mother country "the aliens knew only other aliens." All the Canadian and American intellectuals, those in flight from McCarthy's America and those seeking the roots of their Canadian origin, are merely tourists when they get there. "For even those who had lived in London for years only knew the true life of the city as a rumour."

In this novel Richler places himself in the centre of great world problems. He brings before us the ex-Communist who fled from East Germany, the Ex-Nazi, and a whole assortment of North American fugitives who keep meeting in that vast city as if they were living in a little village where everyone knows everyone else, knows his petty habits and his grand manias. It is a novel in which skill is more in evidence than true passion.

In *The Apprenticeship of Duddy Kravitz* Richler returns to his childhood. He has not yet said all there is to be said. To the bitterness, the surly anger of *Son of a Smaller Hero* is added the dream of a world in which frankness, straightforwardness and love reign together. Great is the disenchantment of the unfortunate child who has put all his hopes in the mystery of non-Jewish society and has found there the same recurring faults as elsewhere.

Duddy Kravitz and his brother are both ambitious; they are children who have emerged from the slum and long to fill their lungs with the air of the great outdoors. One of them wishes to become a possessor, to affirm his power by material conquest. The other thinks to obtain prestige and the respect of Society by his studies and his medical profession. It is a young French-Canadian girl who—for Duddy —symbolizes all the mysterious beauties and inexhaustible enchantments of the unknown world which lies beyond the ghetto. But his unhealthy ambition drives him to destroy the loyal love which gratifies him yet which he can do nothing but annihilate.

His brother gains admittance to a closed circle of Anglo-Saxon Christians. It is a bitter victory, for this world conceals nothing but moral corruption and disintegration. These young people of good family come together in order to drink, and as a sign of friendship they ask of him a service which shows how much they really despise him. They ask him to use his medical knowledge to procure an abortion. The world that is to be encountered outside the walls of the ghetto is hardly a pleasant one.

In this novel, which is without doubt its author's most accomplished work, one can measure his talent against his limitations. Stirred by a demanding passion, he is led to destroy his characters through caricature. Facing a society which he wishes to conquer, he has no time to look at it, to understand it, to perceive its complete ambiguity. His characters are linear, for complexity would deprive them of the artificial consistency which is fabricated by a novelist whose wish to do battle is stronger than his desire to comprehend. This world without love or tenderness is at once sentimental and false—false because sentimental.

Richler manipulates situations and characters to fill a void which no degree of inventiveness can conceal. He does not succeed in breaking the yoke in which his sensibility imprisons him, for he takes no account of the sensibilities of others, and especially of his characters. These are his banner-bearers, the extensions of his own tastes and whims.

It is evident that Richler, who burns with the desire to plunge into the great ocean which he sees beyond the walls of the ghetto, can never quit St. Urbain Street. Whether he walks in England, France or Spain, he carries everywhere his little world, his secret fatherland, for he never succeeds in completing and going beyond his adolescence, which is its product.

In his last novel his choice is made. He is the master of artifice and appearance, and he intends to demonstrate the fact. In fabricating his caricatures he goes to the limit of his powers. He no longer pretends to create living personages or complex situations.

The Incomparable Atuk is a great piece of farce in which the child of the ghetto, once again disguised behind the mask of a fake Eskimo poet, makes his conquest of a world of imposters and hollow men. Richler turns his vengeful anger against all those personalities of swollen reputation and unmerited celebrity who people the intellectual world of Toronto. All of them are provincials puffed up with their false importance, blinded by their degree of influence, corrupted by the ambient complacency. The adolescent who reproached his parents and society in general for responding meagrely to his longing for purity, now directs a burst of mocking laughter against a world which was to blame for the mutilation of his dreams.

The great defeat and the true failure will be those of Richler himself if he has made his long journey merely to resign himself in the end to marching in step in the ranks of that immense army of script-writers from Hollywood and the various Madison Avenues of the world who fill the pages of the popular magazines and put interminable dialogues into the mouths of the protagonists of the soap stories of television. Can he overcome his sensitiveness? Will he be able to outgrow his childhood? Richler, who is still young, might discover in time that the kind of success he obtains will prove ephemeral if the craftsman in him kills the artist. Recognizing the power of American culture is not itself an insurmountable deterrent. After all, he can tread in the paths of Bellow and Malamud instead of those of Jerome Weidman and Herman Wouk.

SOME NOTES ON THE JEWISH NOVEL
IN ENGLISH

or Looking Backward from Exile

LESLIE FIEDLER

"By the rivers of Babylon we sat down and wept . . ." Or so at least it is reported in *the* Book: the first—though by no means the last—of those Jewish books which the non-Jewish world has somehow been persuaded is its book, too. Sat down and wept, to be sure, but sang and wrote too, sang of the weeping, wrote of the singing, thus inventing the first Jewish profession, writing in exile—a permanent Jewish profession everywhere. I had thought it in America, only last year. But this year I have looked about me in search of Jewish writers in England, *real* Jewish writers, who write their Jewishness, however vestigial, and their exile, however cozy; and convince non-Jewish readers that in some sense they are Jews, too, and exiles as well, though they had not suspected it before. And I have found none. No Jewish writers in England. How can it be?

The question troubled me from the start, and so I asked those whom destiny (I have been teaching in an English University all year) had put in my power, my poor captive students. How does it happen, I demanded of them, that there is no serious, no considerable Anglo-Jewish Novel? You share with us Americans a common language, the mother-tongue, in fact, of most living Jews, who once wrote in Aramaic or Arabic or Yiddish or German, but now choose English or American or Anglo-American. Way back at the turn of the century you produced Israel Zangwill, one of the first Jewish writers to adopt the new

From *The Running Man*, Vol. 1, No. 2 (July-August 1968); London, England; pp. 18-21. By permission of the author.

mother tongue. But though in the United States novelists like Bellow and Mailer and Malamud, poets like Allen Ginsberg speak for all Americans, stand at the centre of the scene—almost too established, too successful, so that resentment grows and anti-establishment writers begin to consider them the enemy; nothing remotely similar has happened, is happening here. And why not?

It was a foolish question, perhaps, and so deserved the silence which greeted it, as it greeted most of the misguided American questions I directed at my baffled students in those first weeks. Finally, however, I did get an answer from a girl who, until that point, had always proved more charming than articulate, but was moved at last to say, smiling benignly, "Well—They're All so Rich here. They don't have to write Books, do They?" After which it was my turn to be silent; though I suppose she was really suggesting an answer with her distancing "They" and her off-hand evocation of the envious-spiteful stereotype. Maybe it is essentially that mild-as-milk, matter-of-fact anti-Semitism, which I have found everywhere in England, that has prevented Jews here from becoming spokesmen for anything except their own parochial interests, or, alternatively, slightly quaint entertainers like say, Chaim Bermant.

For better or for worse (so at any rate it seems to me), the Jews in England, quite like the Pakistanis or the Jamaicans, or, for that matter, the Irish, are felt to be English only insofar as they seem to have ceased being Jewish; but this is the absolute opposite of the American case, in which the rule is, has been for a decade or two: the more Jewish, the more American. It is for this reason, then, that the handful of Anglo-Jewish writers of talent actually producing fiction and verse are not felt to add up to anything significant. There are novelists who happen to be Jewish but no Jewish novel.

On the other hand, there is a *female* novel in England, where certain middle-aged women (some of them irrelevantly Jewish) tend to function like certain middle-aged Jews (some of them irrelevantly female) in the United States. I do not read these English ladies often or with much pleasure, but I have enough sense of them to have composed in my head a composite portrait of the typical recent English novelist labelled, for convenience, Muriel Murdoch. And in moments of perversity, I have tried to imagine mating her with her American opposite number, called, of course, Bernard Bellow. They are not utterly unlike, since M.M. shares with B.B. certain memories of the Thirties and World War II, as well as an interest in the language of Existentialism. But her stock-in-trade is her battered sexuality rather than her disappearing ethnic identity; and even if her affairs turn out to be, like his ghetto origins, just another image for alienation, I am afraid I could never get my imaginary couple past the first strains of introduction. Perhaps the true opposite of the Jew is not (as, I seem to recall, Maurice Samuel once suggested) the Gentleman, but the Lady, or, to be quite up-to-date, the ex-Lady; and these opposites do *not* attract.

America has, at any rate, ever since the end of the War against Hitler chosen to identify itself with the Jew—quite disregarding a warning against this rapprochement issued some fifty years ago by D. H. Lawrence, who, however resolutely not a gentleman, was as anti-Semitic as any Englishman. Meanwhile, England has chosen to see itself as the aging lady, which means, I suppose, no match—though a transatlantic offspring is possible all the same; since in the realm of the imagination, even the refusal to mate is not a guaranteed contraceptive. But where could he go, this unwanted child of M.M. and B.B., equally unwelcome at both poles of the English-speaking world, except, perhaps, to the No-man's-Land, the Demilitarized Zone of Canada. But if he were, in fact, there, he would be invisible from South of the Border as well as from the Other Side of the Atlantic—since, despite occasional valiant efforts to *find* Canadian literature (Edmund Wilson pro-vides one notable recent example), it remains stubbornly unavailable to English and American readers alike.

Still, I myself have been reading Canadian books for a long time and have been variously amused, dismayed, interested and bored—but not really moved (even enough to want to register my reactions in print) except by the work of two authors, both self-exiled English-speaking Jews from Montreal, one of whom I have known for a long time now, the other of whom I have come across only quite recently: Mordecai Richler and Leonard Cohen. That they both be Jews is fair enough, proving once more that, culturally speaking, Canada is part of the American rather than the British Commonwealth; and that they have both chosen to exile themselves from their place of birth is appropriate, too, proving once more that the America Canada is really like is always the America of three decades before.

Among us in the United States, exile, particularly to England, seems scarcely a typical strategy these days (imagine Saul Bellow or John Barth or Allen Ginsberg permanently planted in the English countryside); but for Richler it apparently provides the possibility of participating in American culture—contributing to *Commentary,* starring in the first issue of the *New American Review*—without the defensive self-consciousness he would have felt following a similar course at home. From England, at any rate, he seems to be able to join, however belatedly, the extended Norman Podhoretz "family" not as a poor relation from the North, but as a distinguished foster-brother from overseas. And England, in addition, has provided him with a new subject, the subject of exile, latter-day or post romantic exile itself, rescuing him from the need to recapitulate earlier American models. *The Apprenticeship of Duddy Kravitz,* for instance, seemed to me when I first encountered it, hopelessly retrospective for all the talent that went into its making—the sort of fictional study of making it out of the ghetto appropriate for Americans only to the Thirties. *Having* made it was our new subject —and Richler's, too, though he did not seem to know it at the start. Still, there was apparent in him a lust for surreal exaggeration and the grotesque, and an affinity for the atrocious—the dirty joke turned somehow horrific, the scene of terror altered somehow into absurdity—which made him, before he himself knew it, a member of the group later to be labelled Black Humorists.

Satire was his special affinity—not, to be sure, polished and urbane satire, but shrill and joyously vulgar travesty— directed, all the same, against pop culture, on the one hand, and advanced or experimental art on the other: middlebrow satire, in fact, however deliciously gross, an anti-genteel defence of the genteel tradition. It is this which makes Richler so difficult a writer for *me* to come to terms with, and—by the same token—so easy a one for the guardians of official morality to accept. His most recent novel, *Cocksure*, for instance, was simultaneously pub- lished in permissive America and in restrictive England; and though it contains one episode in which it is revealed that a prim and aging school-marm has been blowing the top boys in her class, there has been no protest from an irate British public, and no action from the British courts which recently condemned and banned *Last Exit to Brooklyn*. Part of the explanation for this must be surely that, never mind *how*, the schoolmarm in question is re- establishing discipline and hard work in a formerly pro- gressive school; and no true blue Englishman wants to deny what Richler suggests: better *fellatio* than children's productions of plays by the Marquis de Sade. Besides which, in tone and language and indefinable stance, Richler himself belongs to the world of mass culture (in which he has laboured long, continues to support him- self), so that he seems ultimately—*seems*, I think, rather than is—as harmless as *The Black and White Minstrel Show*.

It is quite another aspect of his work which makes Richler more dangerous than he seems perhaps even to himself: his concern with exile, his compulsion to define all predicaments in terms of that hopelessly Jewish concept, and his implicit suggestion that, after all, we are—everyone of us—Jews. In an oddly uncharacteristic, but to me impressive, book called *A Choice of Enemies* (the structure of which reminds me disconcertingly of Graham Greene), Richler turned his cold satirical eye on certain Hollywood exiles in England, victims of the anti-Communist heresy hunts of the fifties, who, stripped of power and wealth, continue to play the old Machiavellian games which earlier they had carried on behind their mouthing of Communist pieties. And in *The Incomparable Atuk,* he deals with the fate of a Far North Eskimo in the world of Toronto pop culture, moving closer and closer to a level of farce and fantasy whose connections with reality are more like those of a Mack Sennet Comedy than a novel of the late nineteenth or early twentieth century.

The Incomparable Atuk, is not quite a successful book (I notice it is not even included among the earlier Richler books listed opposite the title page of *Cocksure*); but in it Richler seems to have discovered at last where the demands of his real gifts were taking him—toward ultimate, absolute burlesque, i.e., burlesque that includes finally the book itself and its author, the sort of nihilism implicit unawares in all pop art, and consciously exploited in "Pop Art" of which *Cocksure* is an example. But ultimate burlesque requires a sense of the ultimate outsider, the real victim, the true Jew, who—in the realm of Anglo-Saxondom at least—turns out to be the Anglo-Saxon: Richler's poor Mortimer Griffin, a Canadian in the world of Anglo-American TV and films, convinced that the Jews are thicker, the Negroes longer than he, who is cuckolded, sacked and due to be murdered as the book closes. He has discovered before that conclusion that certain powerful Jewish entrepreneurs—in particular a bisexual monster-producer, kept alive with multiple transplants—actually manufacture out of plastic the WASP robots who are the screen idols of the world; and is—naturally enough—taken for mad by those whose peace of mind demands that they believe plastic the ultimate reality. It is a book which seems always on the verge of becoming truly obscene, but stops short, alas, at the merely funny. Yet it is so close, so close—the sort of near miss that leaves permanent damage behind.

Perhaps it is close enough, then. Certainly Richler has come as near to saying how it is with us now when the ultimate exile has proved to be success, as anyone can out of the generation which dreamed that success, at a point when being poor and excluded seemed the only real indignity. Or perhaps it is even possible to say that he has come as near as satire can under any circumstances; since satire is the weapon of one—his deepest self made by a failed father, a deprived childhood—who secretly believes himself weak. . . .

COCKSURE

PHILIP TOYNBEE

Mordecai Richler is a satirist, and therefore a comparatively rare bird in our time. A great many writers toy with satire—insert satirical passages into a non-satirical work, or try to give an edge to farce by offering a satirical interpretation of their buffoonery. But Mr. Richler declares himself a conscious and deliberate satirist from the first page of his new novel—I have read, alas, none of his earlier ones—and he keeps up the satirical pace from start to finish. I found it a very invigorating gallop.

The book turns around the axis of a sinister creation known as the Star Maker—an ancient and ruthless impresario who keeps a train of slaves whose chief function is to provide him with spare parts whenever he needs them. (Mr. Richler has been marvellously lucky in his fortuitous topicality. But he had better not count on Mr. Muggeridge: there are other elements in his book which will displease our old Jeremiah.) The Star Maker is a monstrosity: and his final monstrous act is to have himself fitted out with both male and female genitals, that he may fulfil the instructions of a momentarily audacious attendant to "go fuck yourself!"

But though the Star Maker is a *Californian* enormity, as he should be, the scene of the book is London, and the targets are many and varied. I suppose most of them would come under the general title of "swinging"—the whole frantic roundabout of instant-fashion-change and sexual frenzy. Cushioned as I am by the woods and hills of the

From *London Magazine*, May 1968; pp. 77-79. By permission of *London Magazine*.

Welsh Marches this is a world I know very little about: but reports do occasionally filter through to us, and to judge from these Mr. Richler has chosen a worthy subject. The combination of desperate sophistication and left-wing dogmatism sends a shudder down rural spines; and Mr. Richler's progressive school is a momentous invention. After a performance by the children of Sade's *Philosophie dans le Boudoir* a parents-and-teachers meeting is held: Francis Wharton, the enlightened TV producer, began by saying that he had always voted socialist; he deplored censorship in any shape or form, on either side of the so-called Iron Curtain; Victorian double-standards were anathema to him; but all the same he thought it a bit much that just because his thirteen-year-old daughter was the only girl in the fifth form to stop at petting:

"Shame," somebody called out.
—*heavy* petting—
The objector shrugged, unimpressed.
—was no reason for her to come home with a scarlet T for Tease painted on her bosom.
This brought Lady Gilian Horsham, the Oxfam organizer, to her feet. Lady Horsham wished for more coloured neighbours in Lowndes Square. She had, she said, found the play on the twee side here and there, but, on balance, most imaginative.
"Yes, yes," Dr. Booker interrupted bitingly, "but?"
Lady Horsham explained that her daughter, also in the fifth form, but not so crippingly inhibited as the speaker's child—
"Hear! Hear!"
—had already been to the London Clinic to be fitted with a diaphragm.

Does it go on just a little too long? Hasn't the point been more than adequately made before we get to Lady Horsham at all? Perhaps; but this over-emphasis is a fault common to all but the most crafty of satirists.

Other targets of Mr. Richler's are the aggressive Jewish hunt for anti-Semitism; the cinema industry; publishing, and treating the Germans like human beings. It is unlikely that any reader will share all Mr. Richler's antipathies. For myself I would dearly like to see more coloured neighbours in Lowndes Square, and I find Mr. Richler's attitude to the Germans fairly repulsive. He wrote an article, or letter to an editor about this, some time ago, and I was restrained from writing an angry riposte only by the fact that Mr. Richler is himself Jewish and I am not. But this is not a good enough excuse. Many Jews who were in concentration camps while Mr. Richler was a child in Canada have avoided the unpleasant absurdity of supposing that all Germans are born bad. He should be able to do the same.

And while in a captious mood I would add that a general weakness of this funny and memorable book is that it is quite impossible to detect the moral platform on which Mr. Richler is standing and from which his darts are launched. Nobody wants a satirist to make a solemn declaration of faith, but that declaration is implied by the best satirists in everything they write. Here is a striking example of Mr. Richler's failure: an elderly and highly reputable Canadian governess decides to take a job in the monstrous school, with the intention of counteracting its malignant influence. At first we are led to understand that she is having a great success just because she is introducing discipline, rewards, privacy, etc.—all the things which the school rejects but children need. Not a bit of it. It turns out that she is getting her splendid results simply by rewarding the children with her own techniques of mutual masturbation. Seeing ahead of it the fence of a positive moral judgment, Mr. Richler's horse has shied away from it.

Another sign of the same weakness is that Mr. Richler's unheroic hero, Mortimer Griffin, is not a Candide who is punished by the wicked world for his innocence, but simply a weaker member of the wicked world. Indeed his creator happily joins in pursuing and mocking him to the death.

The weakness is a serious one, and before Mr. Richler writes a really good satire he will have to learn not only what he hates but where he hates it from. Meanwhile *Cocksure* is a highly entertaining book, and often a properly uncomfortable one.

POP STRIP

W. J. IGOE

Ten years ago Mordecai Richler's novel would have been a shocking and sensational publication. Today, I suspect and hope, it will shock no one save Sir Cyril Black and the editors of *Private Eye*.

Judiciously generous in its use of four-letter words, reasonably obsessed by the parts played by genitalia, bosoms, &c., in the western way of life, kindly while unsentimental in its portrayal of liberals, intellectual and slightly moronic, extremely—some might say excessively—funny, its message is very moral. Were Kafka and Nathanael West contemporaries, living at this hour, and they collaborated to write a prose comic strip, something like *Cocksure* might emerge. And yet it is a highly original concoction, a sort of Pop *Pilgrim's Progress* written by a Jewish Bunyan.

Mortimer Griffin, a Canadian, White, Anglo-Saxon and Protestant, is a guilty man. During the war he was awarded the Victoria Cross for saving an n.c.o's life and for this he is exposed on the BBC programme *Insult* as a latent homosexual. His wife, who spends her life washing and fighting anti-racialism, interprets his observations on a virile Jewish colleague as evidence that he is soul-brother to Heinrich Himmler.

Mortimer, in a frenzy of humiliation, builds a reputation for virility by lavish expenditure at a pharmacy next to the office pub: and wonders if Oxfam can find a use for his purchases. Lord Woodcock, proprietor of the Oriole Press, veteran of countless political causes (and Mortimer's

From *The Times*, April 20, 1968, London, England. Reproduced from *The Times Literary Supplement/The Times* by permission.

employer), has promised him the succession, and then, from Las Vegas, the Star Maker reaches out to take over the press. And Mortimer's problems expand to cosmic proportions.

Richler blends Pop science into Pop art in the Star Maker, who has used his wealth to perpetuate his life: "You do worry, you know, when the young fellas begin to go. Churchill, Maugham, Beaverbrook." He likes Mortimer, and the WASP finds a mistress through him, one who "cuts" just at the point where life would not, quite yet, get an X certificate. She had been reared on scenarios. It all ends in a "dissolve," after the WASP discovers the Star Maker's secret—self-propagation and the story of how "Operation Goy-Boy began. . . . There we were, you see, a handful of kikes, dagos and greaseballs, controlling the images Protestant America worshipped."

Were he not quite so obviously sane one might drop another name by writing that Mordecai Richler evokes Dean Swift brooding over Soho at high noon.

WHY, WHY SHOULD MORDECAI BOTHER WITH US AT ALL?

LARRY ZOLF

"Mordecai Richler is a professional Jew," Douglas Fisher, the Friendly Giant of Canadian Socialism, pontificated piously on a TV program recently. A puzzling remark, one that makes this reviewer wonder what there is about Richler that makes him such a burr to Canada's professional bores.

No one, I suppose, would think of calling Doug Fisher a professional radical, the resident pink elephant of a Tory newspaper. One wouldn't I suppose, because most Canadians spend their entire lives without thinking of Doug Fisher at all.

Not so for Mordecai Richler. To be Canadian in any meaningful sense today one must come to grips with what he has to say. To Doug Fisher he may be a "professional Jew," to many Jews he is a "Jewish anti-Semite", to me he is one of the country's best writers and surely one of its most penetrating wits.

Considering the shallowness and hysteria of the attacks frequently levelled at him I sometimes wonder why Richler continues to bother with us at all. Perhaps he should leave Canada to the bores—to Doug Fisher and all those hyper-sensitive professional Jews—the Jewish doctors, lawyers and architects of York Centre—who so recently and decisively rejected Doug Fisher at the polls.

Perhaps the best clue as to the difficulties Richler faces with his fellow Canadians is given by Richler himself. "To be a Jew and a Canadian," he says, "is to emerge from the ghetto twice, for self-conscious Canadians, like some touchy

From the *Toronto Telegram*, November 16, 1968. By permission of *The Telegram*.

Jews, tend to contemplate the world through a wrong-ended telescope."

It is through this kind of telescope that Canadians most frequently view the giant phenomenon to the south of us. While it is true that many members of the Canadian élite differ sharply as to the merits of political and economic continentalism there is one type of continentalism the Canadian illuminati, en masse, are most fanatically opposed to. I refer, of course, (borrowing Richler's own phrase) to "the Jewish cultural take-over" in the United States.

That most distinctive and most influential segment of American culture is not part of the cultural continentalism the Canadian intelligentsia is prepared to buy. In the United States Phillip Roth, Saul Bellow, Norman Mailer, Bernard Malamud, Leslie Fiedler are *American* writers. In Canada Mordecai Richler is "a professional Jew."

In Canada the *good* Jew is a WASP. *Good* Canadian Jews never talk about Jews or being Jewish, don't think Jewish, don't look Jewish. Their noses are bobbed, and their minds are circumcised.

To people like this Mordecai Richler is a menace. They are not amused when in his Catskills essay he reveals the follies and foibles, the warts and vulgarities of their less sophisticated brethren. They feel only anger (alas, no shame) when Richler's piece on Israel reveals some disturbing ironies for our modern times: like the Israeli sabras who say Israeli Arabs "won't mix, stick to their own people and areas" and have "loyalties outside the country"; or the Israeli death-camp survivor who admits that Arab refugee camps are deplorable but insists Dachau was worse.

What is really sad is what those Canadians who shout "professional Jew" and "Jewish anti-Semite" at a man of Richler's obvious talents, reveal about themselves and this country. What seems to link both these groups together is paranoia, a sense of inferiority, a feeling of alienation. The Canadian WASP élite is essentially cut off from the superior cultures of their American and British counterparts. Years ago it was a direct and vital part of the British Empire. It was getting part of the action. Being British was enough. The demise of the British Empire and non-membership in the new American one has left our WASP élite homeless, ghettoized, so to speak, in the northern half of the American continent.

It's not surprising they would pass this sense of frustration and alienation on to the Canadian Jewish community, itself ghettoized, and cut-off from its culturally superior counterparts in Britain and the U.S.A. Canadian Jewry is certainly the most alienated Jewish community in the English-speaking world. It's surely a typical Canadian irony that one-half of the tiny Jewish community in this country should live in Montreal and be English-speaking, making it in a French city a kind of ghetto minority squared.

It is doubly ironic that the Montreal Jewish Community should look to that city's WASP élite for inspiration and leadership. It is one beleaguered minority leading another in a basically hopeless situation. It is not surprising that the paranoia gauge of Canada's Jewish community, with its Montreal base and leadership is high; nor is it surprising that its toleration of self-criticism, no matter how skilfully and accurately done, is low. A Richler poking fun at Catskill absurdities in the United States would draw little attention. A Richler doing it here is inevitably a "Jewish anti-Semite".

Vel, anyway, all I can say, is Tanks Gods, for Mordecai Richler. He is a bad Jew and a worse Canadian but he tells it as it is. In *Hunting Tigers Under Glass,* a collection of his essays and reports, Richler writes about bad Jews and worse Canadians, superbly.

Take for example his hilarious account of that peculiar Canadian psycho-drama, the annual gathering of the Canadian Authors' Association. Listed by Richler as being in attendance, were such literary lights as Bluebell Phillips, Phoebe Erskine Hyde, and Una Wardelworth. Overlooked, much to my annoyance, were authors Carpathia Radish, Hathaway Yoyo, Paisley Goornisht, and Gay Abandon (she of Memoirs Of A Venetian Streetwalker fame).

Mentioned by Richler, as if in passing, was the Canadian literary hit of EXPO year, *Ripe And Ready*. Sad to say, this was not a Canadian *Fanny Hill* but rather a history of the Canadian apple. Unforgivably ignored by Richler were such Canadian literary hits of yesteryear as *Awake And Sing,* a history of the Canadian Opera Company; *Hail and Farewell,* a history of Canadian crop failures; and *From See To See,* a history of Canadian Catholic voyeurs.

Equally unforgivable in Richler is his tendency, at times, to view us provincial Canadians with the lofty disdain of the profligate, world-weary sophisticate. Air Canada does, after all, fly across the pond; the *Paris* and *Partisan Reviews* do find their way into the occasional household; the ladies from Dubuque and Coronation Street utter the same banalities as Anne of Green Gables.

Less irritating but a bit unnerving is Richler's tendency to drop the names of good friends and potential employers in some of his reports and essays. More disturbing is Richler's barely suppressed desire to be Canada's Edmund Wilson. His serious comments on writers and writing, film-making and politics are insightful and often valuable, but for the most part, are prissy and professorial in tone, often indistinguishable from the many academic prigs that already clutter up the field in these areas.

God forbid I should be labelled a professional Jew, but I like Richler best when he is idiosyncratic and auto-biographical, first-person and Jewish. Two of his essays in this collection "The Great Comic Book Heroes," and "Jews In Sport" are comic classics of our time.

Did you know that the Green Hornet had his origins in Hassidic mythology, that Jay Garrick, the Flash, was Jewish but Reform, and that Clark Kent is "the archetypal middle-class WASP"?

Did you know that Kermit Kitman was the first Jew in Canadian professional baseball, that he was a good fielder but a lousy hitter, suffering from the dread Jewish disease of over-compensation? Or that Hyman Cohen pitched seven games for the Chicago Cubs in 1955, winning none and losing none? How about the Jewish Texan, Steve Allan Herz, who played five games in 1964 for Houston, compiling a batting average of .000?

WOW! All this you've seen and heard right here, live for the first time folks, in *Hunting Tigers Under Glass*.

The final words on *Hunting Tigers Under Glass* should go to Richler. Says he: "If I'm able to communicate just some of my enjoyment of Israel, the Catskills, comicbooks, Jews in sport and the Canadian comedy, to readers, then I will count this collection a success."

Well start counting, Mordecai. It's a success, it's a success!! Me, I can hardly wait for the movie!

ON THE BLOCK

MORDECAI RICHLER: *Hunting Tigers Under Glass*

Mr. Richler has collected together a bundle of essays, reports and reviews on a variety of topics not immediately likely to fit together: Canada and sport, various forms of pop literature and art, Jewish-American writing, and Israel. The focus is Mordecai Richler himself. "After all, I'm a Jewish writer from Canada," he says. But so is Saul Bellow [sic]; and the book, on internal evidence alone, is not by him. The pieces, bitter-sweet and often very funny, form a kind of instant biography of reminiscence, observation and opinion: even when writing a fictional review of Malamud or Mailer, Mr. Richler usually turns the occasion into one for idiosyncrasy and recollection.

Moreover, they are written from a number of wry angles, some of them coming from Mr. Richler's intelligently common sense radical view of two forms of provincialism he knows very well indeed, the Jewish and the Canadian: and some from the fact that for a Jewish novelist he has taken the unpredictable tack of finding his cosmopolis not in New York but in London. More still come from the fact that the pieces address heterodox reading-publics, some were directed at American general audiences *(Holiday)*, some for American intellectual audiences *(New York Review of Books)*, some for Jewish-American intellectual audiences *(Commentary)*, some for Anglo-American intellectual audiences *(Encounter)*, and some for English readers *(London Magazine)*. Experts in

From the *Times Literary Supplement*, January 23, 1969, London, England. Reproduced from *The Times Literary Supplement/The Times* by permission.

tone will be interested in determining the differences and the complexity of Mr. Richler's consequent culture.

It all seems to go to show that it is, as they say, hard to know who one is nowadays: but actually Mr. Richler knows very well. He is a confessed product of the 1940s, when one was interested in pop not because it was camp but because it was what there was, just as he says as a student he and his friends had sex in the afternoon not because they were radical or alienated but because they were horny. Anyone who has followed out the earlier fortunes of these pieces, his review of Edmund Wilson's *O Canada* or of Feiffer's *Comic Book Heroes* will know with what confident opinionation he cuts through the glossy romanticisms and belaboured intellectual worries in the interests of establishing the real feel of the thing.

The three essays on Canada and Canadianism here (while not as good as his brilliant treatment of the same thing in his novel *The Apprenticeship of Duddy Kravitz*) have some of the best insights into provincial cosmopolitanism, mainly because Mr. Richler observes, collects and remembers the essential data with at once an ironic and a sympathetic vision. The basic tactic of compassion and irony is very funny and it brings him right into the middle of the enclaves of *kitsch*. It is similarly applied to the Jewish resort area of the Catskills, that fascinating Sullivan county hinterland where Jewish entertainment and high-living thrive ("Lou Goldstein, the Director of Daytime Social Activities [at Grossinger's], was running his famous game of Simon Says on the terrace"). And it is finally brought right home to what for Mr. Richler must be the heart of it all, Israel, in a sharp travel piece that captures all the classic reversals (including being told: "The trouble with the Arabs is they won't mix. They're private. They stick to their own people and areas").

The targets are never *too* easy since Mr. Richler is fully involved—as the Canadian-Jewish good-bad boy of the 1940s who himself went through both the bourgeois and the intellectual apprenticeship. The pieces on comic book heroes, sport and films all hark back to that apprenticeship. Writing on Mailer, he picks up and applies Baldwin's phrase about him as "the toughest kid on the block." The kids on the block and what became of them through the past twenty years of complex history really form the theme that runs behind these pieces. The time is one in which it became easier to be a Jew (and Mr. Richler is excellent on the inept touchiness of hard-core Jewish culture, which he has constantly offended). As one of the staff at Grossinger's where Eddie Fisher was discovered, tells him; " 'If you had told me in those days that Fisher would get within ten feet of Elizabeth Taylor—' He stopped short, overcome. 'The rest,' he said, 'is history.' "

But easier can be harder. Mr. Richler is a writer of ironies, detachment, and comic involvements rather than a voice of exile or anomaly; but one can see in his writings why the Jewish writer or intellectual might have gone a good deal deeper into self-doubt. In a critically sharp review of Malamud's *The Fixer*, he points out the way in which the Jewish writer tends, his modern experience being now pretty well on file in the Jewish-American efflorescence of the 1950s, to hark back to origins, to the *shtetl* or the archetypal pogrom. Mr. Richler himself holds to the fascination of ordinary origins, and comes out as a grand supra-provincial. That, perhaps, is why he takes as the real clue to the meaning of the Superman comic strip—which turns Clark Kent, the provincial square, into an invincible hero—the fact that it was invented by a Canadian Jew.

This is a lively book, the more illuminating if you consider Mordecai Richler, and he goes on giving us more and more grounds for thinking so, an important novelist. And it is a usefully oblique insight into a body of experience that the Jewish-American novelists have gone through with more tension and bravura, but with a good deal less irony and humour.

A SURVEY OF RICHLER'S FICTION

HUGO MCPHERSON

. . . The uniqueness of Mordecai Richler (b. 1931) is easy to explain. Like Thoreau, who decided that Harvard taught all the branches of knowledge but none of the roots, Richler wants to get at the prime meaning of experience —to drive life into a corner and see whether it is a good thing or bad. But Richler does not live at Walden; his reality lies somewhere beneath the encrusted hypocrisies and orthodoxies of urban culture; and though in burrowing towards this reality he is often naïve, cranky, and even short-sighted, he is determined (in the words of his best critic, Peter Scott) "to keep to the experience at hand and to the truth which is available." Far from the reflective or analytical mood that has been characteristic of Canadian fiction, Richler's spirit resembles that of the "angry" young Englishman and the "beat" writers of "the great American night"; but though, like them, he strips away the world's pretences, he does not end as an outsider, in alienated or intoxicated freedom. Richler belongs (as Brian Moore does) in society, and he has enough nerve to refuse alienation. If orthodox frauds reject him, he will simply bypass them and create his own order—a crude one, perhaps, but bracing in its directness, and electric with energy.

Since 1954, when he was twenty-two, Richler has produced a tide of film and television scripts, short stories, articles for British, American, and Canadian journals, and

From "Fiction: 1940-1960"; in *Literary History of Canada: Canadian Literature in English*, ed. Carl F. Klinck, et al; University of Toronto Press, 1965; pp. 713-715. By permission of the author and the publisher.

four novels which, though flawed individually, constitute in sum the most promising *œuvre* of the recent period. *The Acrobats* (1954) and *Son of a Smaller Hero* (1955) might both be described as "first novels"; both deal with a hero obsessed by self and in reckless opposition to a world which is stifling, corrupt, and Protean in its deceit. *The Acrobats* recounts the spiritual agony and eventual death of André Bennett, a young Canadian painter in Spain—the symbolic arena of shattered ideals, lost causes, and vain hopes. In this shadowy post-war limbo, Richler's hero learns two truths: "that the poor should have more because they were human and no human should be ugly"; and that the individual must act on what he knows, for "not to act would mean nonliving." Yet when André does act—striking out drunkenly against the ugliness of a former Nazi officer—he is destroyed. He succumbs because of his inexperience, but he does act; and the novel ends in a symbolic birth. André's mistress bears a child (fathered by the Nazi)whom she names André; then, counselled by a sage and benevolent restaurateur, Chaim, she embarks for a new life in America. As Chaim, the humanitarian whose passport is revoked by state after state, affirms: "There is always hope. . . . There has to be."

The forced symbolism of this ending is only one of *The Acrobats'* shortcomings: the festival of San José glitters like the fireworks which conclude it, but falls short of the structural significance which similar rites achieve in Hemingway or Mann; the narrative method flickers uncertainly because the narrator is not sufficiently distinct from his hero; and the echoes of Hemingway, Sartre, and others are more often reflexes than conscious devices. But though the book is not, as one critic claims, "a guide to intelligent, contemporary pastiche," it has a nervous, exploratory power.

Son of a Smaller Hero (1955) is in effect an earlier chapter in fictional autobiography. But if Richler is on firmer ground in the Jewish community of Montreal than he was in Spain, he is still uncomfortably close to his hero's anger and confusion; the family and community described come magnificently to life, but the hero, Noah Adler, is such an unreliable guide to his own experience that the closing ambiguity of the novel appears inadvertent rather than deliberate. The step from this to *A Choice of Enemies* (1957) and *The Apprenticeship of Duddy Kravitz* (1959) is the enormous stride from denial to assertion, from rejection to deliberate choice. As in battle, the technical units lag behind the attack forces in both of these works, but the objectives are taken and held. In *A Choice of Enemies*, the hero is a left-wing expatriate, Norman Price, who has sought refuge in London's Hampstead bohemia, only to discover that his friends, Fifth Amendment heroes (mostly writers and film-makers) are no less ignoble than their bourgeois enemies, and perhaps even more exclusive in their group orthodoxy. As in *The Acrobats*, the central problem concerns a Nazi (this time a refugee from East Germany). In the course of defending this young man's right to strip off the labels with which society has marked him, Norman clashes with his friends and is himself stripped of every mark of prestige which he had enjoyed as an insider. In the nuclear age, Norman realizes, the real enemies are not communism, fascism, or capitalism but the ancient scourges of pride, covetousness, and the lust for power. Finally, after an attack of amnesia (the symbol is awkward) Norman "dies into life"; he chooses to marry a very ordinary English girl and to return to disinterested scholarship; to live not for prestige or power but for unheroic, humane values. Then, sensing perhaps a hint of complacency in this easy-difficult choice, Richler gives the reader a final jab: Norman's "ordinary" wife, it appears, is dazzled by the prestige of his former friends, and begins ingratiating herself with them even before the honeymoon begins.

In *A Choice of Enemies,* Richler the film-writer occasionally interferes with Richler the novelist; suspense is introduced whether meaning requires it or not, and dialogue is often geared to the film editor's cut. In *The Apprenticeship of Duddy Kravitz* the novelist is again in control, but a new problem, the relation between realism and comedy or farce, presents itself. Duddy's apprenticeship—his chequered progress from a Montreal slum to a shaky status as landowner—is a story by turns comic, pathetic, bawdy, and farcical; and though the exuberant reality of Duddy himself is never in doubt, the modulation of other characters from pathos to farce makes the reader's suspension of disbelief something less than willing. But these flaws are principally evidence of the rapidity of Richler's artistic development. The theme of *Duddy Kravitz* extends the quest for values of the earlier books, but this time Richler dares a hero whose background is hard knocks and whose only capital is his ability to charm, twist, dream, calculate, and work. And since Duddy has none of the training or experience of Norman Price, the ironies of his experience are presented without comment; everything is kaleidoscopic, headlong action, and everything is indispensable to the total statement. Hacking his way through the urban jungle of hypocrisy and chicane, Duddy outsmarts enemies and exploits friends, but he finally gets his land, an untouched tract of lake and fields in a high Laurentian valley. In doing so he has sacrificed the respect of his *zeyda* and his sweetheart; both are worthy people, but their codes would bind Duddy permanently in the nightmare of modern urban life. Thus the conclusion of Duddy's ascent is a beginning rather than an end; unlike Nick Garraway of *The Great Gatsby,* however, he possesses not a corrupt Long Island but a virgin tract of Canada from which he raucously dismisses his deformed and vicious rival, Dingleman. Richler does not pose a final question, but one hangs in the air: Will Duddy reproduce on his own land the nightmare which he has escaped?

Mordecai Richler has asked piercing questions on issues which involve the self, the nation, and mankind, and he has dismissed the stock replies that religion, politics, and the polite social sciences and humanities customarily offer. His exuberant style and intellectual toughness make him the most exciting and promising of Canada's younger novelists. . . .

BOOKS BY MORDECAI RICHLER

NOVELS

The Acrobats (1954)
Son of a Smaller Hero (1955)
A Choice of Enemies (1957)
The Apprenticeship of Duddy Kravitz (1959)
The Incomparable Atuk (1963)
Cocksure (1968)

COLLECTION OF STORIES

The Street (1969)

COLLECTION OF ESSAYS

Hunting Tigers Under Glass (1968)

Stories and fragments of novels by Mordecai Richler have been published in:

New Statesman; Canadian Literature; Kenyon Review; The Montrealer; Tamarack Review; The Spectator; New American Review; Maclean's; Modern Occasions; Gentleman's Magazine; The Running Man; Paris Review; Encounter.

Essays and reviews by Mordecai Richler have appeared in:

The Spectator; New Statesman; Twentieth Century; The Montrealer; New American Review; New York Review of Books; Commentary; Book World; New Leader; Holiday; Encounter; London Magazine; The Observer; Manchester Guardian; London Sunday Times; London Sunday Telegraph; Maclean's; Saturday Night.

Television and radio scripts by Mordecai Richler:

A Friend of the People, a TV play for BBC and ITV in England.

Paid In Full, a TV play for ITV in England (also produced on German TV).

A TV adaptation of *Duddy Kravitz* for the Canadian Broadcasting Corporation.

A TV adaptation of his own story "Some Grist for Mervin's Mill," for ITV in England (also produced on German, Swedish and Australian TV).

A TV adaptation of Isaac Babel's story, "Sunset," for the Canadian Broadcasting Corporation. (co-author)

A radio adaptation of his own story, "It's Harder to Be Anybody," for the CBC and the BBC third program.

Film scripts by Mordecai Richler:

No Love for Johnny (co-author)

Life at the Top (sole author)

Translations of Mordecai Richler's novels into other languages:

The Acrobats (into Swedish, Norwegian, Danish and German)

Son of a Smaller Hero (into German)

A Choice of Enemies (into German and French)

The Apprenticeship of Duddy Kravitz (into French, Italian and Hebrew)

Cocksure (into German and Italian)